Hope, Make, Heal

HOPE, MAKE, HEAL

20 Crafts to Mend the Heart

Maya Pagán Donenfeld

ROOST BOOKS

Boulder

2016

Roost Books
An imprint of Shambhala Publications, Inc.
4720 Walnut Street
Boulder, Colorado 80301
roostbooks.com

9 8 7 6 5 4 3 2 1

First Edition
Printed in the United States of America

☯This edition is printed on acid-free paper that meets
the American National Standards Institute z39.48 Standard.
♻Shambhala Publications makes every effort to print on recycled paper.
For more information please visit www.shambhala.com.

Distributed in the United States by Penguin Random House LLC
and in Canada by Random House of Canada Ltd

Designed by Daniel Urban-Brown

Library of Congress Cataloging-in-Publication Data

Donenfeld, Maya Pagán.
Hope, make, heal: 20 crafts to mend the heart/Maya Pagán Donenfeld.
pages   cm
ISBN 978-1-61180-200-9 (pbk.: alk. paper)
1. Handicraft—Therapeutic use. 2. Handicraft—Psychological aspects.
3. Functional foods. 4. Cooking, American.
5. Indians of North America—Food. 6. Traditional medicine. I. Title.
RM735.7.H35D66 2015
745.5—dc23
2014042688

For my mother, who always modeled acceptance of challenges
and embracing them as opportunities for growth.

Hope is the thing with feathers
That perches in the soul,
And sings the tune without the words,
And never stops at all,

And sweetest in the gale is heard;
And sore must be the storm
That could abash the little bird
That kept so many warm.

I've heard it in the chillest land,
And on the strangest sea;
Yet, never, in extremity,
It asked a crumb of me.

—EMILY DICKINSON

CONTENTS

ACKNOWLEDGMENTS

A community of amazing people near and far made it possible for me to write this book. I will be forever grateful to each and every one that offered the kind of inspiration and kindness that helps move mountains. I am especially grateful to the following people:

Jenn Urban-Brown—for providing the wisdom and sharp eye one can only dream of finding in an editor.

Linda Rogharr—for acting as my compass, always guiding me in the right direction.

Laura Nelkin—for simply being my rock, which isn't so simple.

Pixie Lighthorse—for helping me to find the light at the end of each tunnel.

Dawn Grover—for remaining available at any given moment, for whatever was called for.

Karin Suskin—for listening deeply and inspiring me to live from a place of compassion.

Ellen Abrams—for teaching me how to breathe and pause.

Casey Benson, Dani DiCiaccio, and Jung Eun Lee—for offering their beautiful presence to grace some of these pages.

My grandmother, Bev—for teaching me to believe in my worth, never to give up hope, and to hold my head up high.

My mom—for showing me what wonderful mothering really looks like.

Noemi and Sylvan—for giving me the best reasons for learning to heal fully and love unconditionally.

Murillo—for standing by my side and cheering me forward one page at a time.

FOREWORD

A river has a magnificent capacity to carve deep canyons, trickle over rocks, plunge over falls, and keep moving. The river goes where she is meant to, all the while honoring her honest purpose: to ease gracefully over and around the obstacles she encounters. The promise is that if she stays in flow, she will get to where she's going. When words fail us, brought on by deep pain through trauma and loss—from betrayal, disappointment, frustration, grief, anger—our task is to find our way back to the river of our lives. *Making* allows for flow when the heart is tempted to shrink back, stagnate, and wither. When there are no conversations to be had or no comfort is to be found, working with our hands is always available to us and can be a powerful way to help us move forward.

Making as a form of healing has always been present in my life. I watched my grandmother make quilts as far back as my memory can take me. I remember sitting on her bed as a child—tacking yarn with fat, blunt, shiny needles strewn about—my tiny brown legs weighed down by five or six of her quilts. Each of the stitches and patterns told the complicated story of her hard life—and of her love of color and joy, too. Losing a young daughter led her to seek comfort and faith in making what would become warm heirlooms handed down within the family. It was all she could do: sit at her machine, late into the night, thick glasses perched on her nose, making patchwork blocks. It would be many years later that I would puzzle out that her acts of creation were facilitating her transcendence of the pain of loss. In the middle of the mighty confusion of grief, she intuited how to reconnect with the sacred.

I have asked myself how the sacred can reside in the heart when the pain of loss overwhelms it. Through my own traumatic losses—of numerous pregnancies and my marriage of sixteen

years—I have learned to do what my grandmother did: to make until I can hear the sacred whispering to me again. The quiet process of making something helps me pause and acknowledge the thoughts and fears swirling through my body and mind like the eddies of a river. In easing my paintbrush over the canvas, clacking my knitting needles together, and therapeutically punching down the dough, not only do I begin to acknowledge and release what was being felt in my time of ordeal, but I am also able to hear the sacred over the blinding rush of tears and my own wise voice emerging in new form. Creating meaningfully keeps my heart open and alive and always brings me back to a deep appreciation for the strength in my own honest vulnerability.

Maya, too, understands the power of making and has led classes on creating things with our hands to mend our hearts. We met years ago when we roomed together at Squam Art Workshops, and we quickly fell into flow with each other's path. Her students were transforming with craft, and I was able to witness the hope that Maya brought to them through their own acts of remembering that allowed them to weave their feelings of the past into the new shape of who they were becoming. It was a profound and beautiful week that led to many more years of making and healing, and ultimately to this book.

Hope, Make, Heal is a collection of ideas made manifest to stir the heart that is hungry for mending. It was written by the hand of a woman who is like a river, who has kept the magic and mystery of her hands flowing, making meaningful and medicinal crafts for her own soul in transition. Its pages and projects were created as an offering of hope for you, a remembering, and a healing balm.

—PIXIE LIGHTHORSE

We looked into each other and realized that we all share the same river. It flows beneath us and through us, from one dry heart to the next. We share the same river. . . . We may speak different languages and live very different lives, but when that deep water swells to the surface, it pulls us to each other.

—MARK NEPO, *The Book of Awakening*

INTRODUCTION

I was always taught to look for the gifts in everything—to search for silver linings and believe in miracles. It was good training for the morning when my world turned upside down. A sudden and unexpected ending to my marriage of sixteen years thrust me into a world of pain and confusion I had only read about in books and seen in movies. I had experienced hardship—no one gets through four decades without his or her share—but this was trauma like nothing I had felt before. I needed more than an optimistic outlook. My lifeline was positivity. But no one told me how much strength it takes to hold on to it.

When we grieve, statistics and facts feel especially sterile. Most of us reach for the steady hand of another and the faithful ears of loved ones. But even if we're blessed with an understanding community, a deep sense of isolation comes with tragedy. No one else stands in our shoes. Only we will wake up to a new day still facing a life that is altered and shaped by the present loss flowing through us. Rarely is there another person who can understand just what it means to be you. I turned to "experts" and read everything I could find to help me cope with the overwhelming devastation I felt. By the side of my bed was a constantly rotating stack of self-help and spirituality books. It often stood a few feet tall. Many of these volumes became my companions—traveling in my suitcase or riding next to me in the car. Even when I wasn't reading them, I found comfort in their titles and soothing covers. I think I loved them most for the empty space they filled. They kept me company—especially during the long nights when I searched for sleep.

However, I kept feeling that one book was missing. The one that spoke about what to do—not just what I was feeling and thinking, but how to focus and channel my powerful flood of emotions into something I could see and touch. I am an artist and a maker. I know how busy hands can profoundly nurture a heart and stop a head from spinning. During this time, creating something beautiful and expressive took on a new dimension as I tried to mend my broken parts by making something to wear, carry, touch, and gaze upon. My state of mind couldn't handle complicated instructions, nor did I have the patience to learn something too new or challenging. I just yearned to create things that were simple, intentional, and most of all, meaningful.

Hope, Make, Heal is the book I wish someone had given me. It merges hope and creativity so that we can find renewal and restoration during life's transitions and after deep loss. It grew out of a longing for peace and the universal need for something tangible to hold on to. Every project within these pages comes from my own survival toolbox. Many of the ideas were birthed during the most tender and vulnerable times in my life. And I know that they work. I've experienced how they comfort and support and have witnessed the impact they have on the maker and those around them. This book is a resource for personal healing and a gift for your friend in need.

Hope, Make, Heal contains four sections: Wounded, Synchronicity, Healing, and Reinvention. Each contains five items to make, plus a nourishing recipe. Each section also includes a guided meditation contributed by Ellen Abrams, my dear and wise friend who leads the weekly Mindfulness through Trauma meditation group I attend. I have found a regular meditation practice to be an anchor during the work of everyday living and an invaluable tool in the process of healing from grief. It is an invitation to quiet the mind and allow space for being present in the moment. Practicing this stillness and cultivating an awareness of what is real in the *here and now* is just like exercising a muscle. A regular workout keeps this meditation muscle strong so that we are prepared and able to stay present when a crisis derails us instead of remaining trapped in yesterday or grasping for the unknown of tomorrow.

Writing is another powerful instrument that supports well-being. Finding words to name our feelings and experiences organizes our thoughts and helps us find meaning when answers are out of reach. At the beginning of each project, I have included a Heart Prompt to focus on and contemplate. I encourage you to write down in the Open-Heart Journal what impressions and ideas the Heart Prompts kindle. An affirmation is offered with each project as well. These "I am" statements are assertions that something exists or is true. Affirmations have been shown to bring about significant shifts in how we perceive ourselves. By repeating them or placing them in high-traffic spots in our home, we can surround ourselves with positive thinking, which has the ability to increase favorable changes in our view of self and life.

While there was deliberateness around the placement of every component of this book, each person's process will be as unique as her or his story. Some may want a slow, cover-to-cover read; others will instantly be making the Survival Satchel in the very last section. Have faith in your ability to know exactly what you need. Even if you're not accustomed to listening to that wise voice inside, it never stops whispering; pausing and trusting that voice helps to turn up the volume.

Although the premise of this book is self-care through creativity, that doesn't mean you must craft alone. Many of the projects would be wonderful to do with family and friends. Most materials and tools can be found around the house or close by with little effort or money spent. Even the stitching crafts can all be done by hand; it isn't necessary to use a sewing machine. The focus is on ease and accessibility, so previous skills aren't needed. The beauty of the projects' simplicity also means that making multiples isn't so daunting.

Sometimes it's hard to know the right thing to say when someone you love is struggling. Many of these projects are meaningful offerings that speak louder than words. They link us to one another with the unspoken eloquence of true understanding. The relationships formed or strengthened during stressful times are often connections of depth and transparency. We seek out people who are not afraid to witness our pain and do not ask us to wear a mask of pretense. We are all connected in our humanity and our suffering. And so you've picked up this book because your river flows directly into mine. We share the same river, you and I.

WOUNDED

And you would accept the seasons of your heart,
even as you have always accepted the seasons
that pass over your fields.
And you would watch with serenity
through the winters of your grief.

—KAHLIL GIBRAN, *The Prophet*

I NTENSE SORROW WILL STRIKE EACH OF US at some point in our life. It often claims us with an overwhelming force that knocks us to our knees and throws us to the ground. When one is struck with this kind of sorrow and such intense feelings, it can be shocking. I was astonished at how powerfully painful a shattered heart truly was. Initially, I thought I might be so consumed by agony that my body would shut down and I'd surely die. I remember moments when I was alone in my house and my despair felt so heavy that I had no choice but to collapse on the floor beneath its weight. Some moments I even had trouble breathing and found myself gasping for air. It was as if there were never enough oxygen in the room. In listening to others share their unique stories, I recognized the common thread in many of our initial responses to trauma: a physical and mental agony that devours any sense of our prior reality. The only thing that exists is the moment we are experiencing. The only thing we can clearly see, taste, touch, or hear is our suffering.

In the early days of sorrow, our perception of time is impacted as well. Minutes can drag on like days, and afternoons can slip by without our even knowing where they've vanished. In grief's wake, reality is deeply distorted, and we all tick to a surreal clock. Salvador Dalí's most familiar work, *The Persistence of Memory,* becomes the landscape of our days. I've spoken to many about this altered state and have found that the walking wounded indeed reside together among the soft and melted pocket watches of our collective experience of pain.

During this time of sorrow I often felt that I was slower. It was as if my internal "gears" hadn't been wound up properly and my heart had stopped beating in its regular rhythm. For many, a deceleration happens, allowing ample space for processing and assimilating pain. We slow down simply without choice. Some do just the opposite. A good friend, whose husband passed away suddenly, said that she speeded up in order not to have room in her day for the pain. Slow or swift, our relationship with the passing of time is influenced deeply during a crisis and its aftermath. Keeping this in mind is important—for all of us and for those supporting us. Our pendulum will swing back and forth, slowly righting itself in accordance with the rest of the world as we move forward.

The same survival instincts that make us recoil from bodily harm are triggered by emotional distress. It's a reflex—similar to the response that we have when we touch a hot stove. Our natural tendency is to try to escape the pain. This denial helps us to superficially maintain our routines and care for our families while in crisis, but it doesn't serve us in the long run.

Ignored wounds rarely heal. They often fester, only to reveal themselves later in chronic illness, depression, anxiety, and unhealthy lifestyles. It's natural to feel helpless in the midst of the unforeseen, but we do have a choice in how we respond. If we can recognize this new opportunity to redesign the life still in front of us, rather than be crippled by something we couldn't control, we move into an accelerated growth spurt. So often we hear people say that it was a life-threatening disease or traumatic divorce that ended up being the greatest gift of all. It is in the death of something or someone that we are pushed beyond our limits. This is the hardest work there is, but after the crash and burn, something beautiful is often born out of the ashes.

The first step is to acknowledge the hurt of our situation and mourn fully. Whatever the loss, we long for what was, how it used to be, or how it was supposed to be according to our carefully laid plans. Accepting and staying awake to our feelings take practice. Every new day is an opportunity to exercise the ability to stay present. Our self-awareness will grow, and with it comes an understanding of the world around us. Those having labored through a dark time often have a deeper appreciation for beauty, love, and those perfect small moments that count so much more than we previously realized.

Making sense of what we're experiencing diffuses some of its mystery and weakens its ability to shake our souls. Although the way we process pain is very personal and individual, there are several typical ways that many of us experience a great loss. Elisabeth Kübler-Ross, a Swiss American psychiatrist, discussed the five stages of grief in her book *On Death and Dying*. Although she wrote the book back in 1969, her work with terminally ill patients is still relevant today, and *On Death and Dying* is widely used by therapeutic professionals as a model of how people respond to any traumatic crisis. She categorized these five stages of grief:

1. *Denial.* Often the first reaction, as mentioned previously, is to shut out the reality of the present situation.
2. *Anger.* Fury around the injustice of it all can be very consuming and manifests itself in outrage with oneself, those close to us, and even a higher power.
3. *Bargaining.* In the hope of negotiating a different outcome, we often proclaim, "I'll do anything if . . ."; rarely are these terms sustainable.
4. *Depression.* When sadness ultimately sinks in, the situation has finally been assessed for what it is. This is when people often check out and detach themselves from others. The emotional gravity is so painful that tears remain on the surface and weeping is unavoidable.
5. *Acceptance.* Typically a sense of calm comes with surrendering to what is, as well as clarity about what's possible and what hasn't yet arrived.

These stages do not always follow a linear path, though. There will be some circling and cycling through each one before healing starts to settle in.

It is in this chapter that I invite you to wrap yourself in all of your feelings and own them. The projects here encourage you to embrace your wounds fully and to recognize the sacredness that partners with darkness. The journal records your experience in words and pictures; it honors this journey as one worth documenting. The altar invites reflection at a time when the doorway to a spiritual practice is open widest. Making your own candles will help you to remember that there is light at the other end of the tunnel. A sleep potion can be created to help you find the rest so needed right now. Cocoon yourself from the world and nurse your sadness without guilt. Everyone deserves this space to feel freely without censure.

Before you begin the projects in this chapter, I encourage you to give yourself the gift of quiet time. Setting aside ten to fifteen minutes of sitting in stillness with an intention of self-compassion can have a lasting impact on how you relate to your pain. The mind hungers for this kind of relief in the same way that a heart aches for solace.

With gentle attention, sit comfortably yet upright. With intention, take several deep breaths and then allow your breath to be natural. See what it is like to relax as much as possible. Soften at the eyes. Try on a smile at the eyes and the mouth, re-verberating down to the heart. A smile, even a slight upturn at the mouth, gives our nervous system an invitation to relax.

Chest open, belly soft, let your awareness return again and again to the sensations of your breath—the inflow and outflow. Let this breath be a kind of home base, a gateway to being here.

We begin with the invitation to connect to what is actually here—the simple and yet not so simple task of making room for ourselves. Connecting again and again in each moment, to embrace what is actually so, to make space for what is here in this heart. Sometimes when we get quiet, what we notice is the depth of pain we are carrying. Pain has the ability to grab hold like a vise-grip. There are times when it winds so tightly and completely that it shapes everything within our inner and outer vision. The only way to endure, and potentially transform what is painful, is to experience all that we actually feel. Perhaps it is easier with a gentle hand over your heart (try this now)—not to cover over anything, but simply to make room for what is there. Imagine the possibility of not opposing what is inside yourself but finding a way to feel at home within yourself, even when home hurts.

What happens when we can acknowledge our woundedness and connect directly to what is right here and now? We can learn to be with what is actually so. When we pause the story of what we think is happening, we open ourselves to what is *truly* happening in this moment, underneath the hand that rests on our heart.

When we drop from virtual reality, which is only our constructed narrative of ourselves, to actual reality we tap into a moment-to-moment and ever-changing constellation of sounds, sensations, and noticing. We connect with ourselves, our tender, shaky, and wounded human selves. Trusting the waves of hereness is the doorway to aliveness.

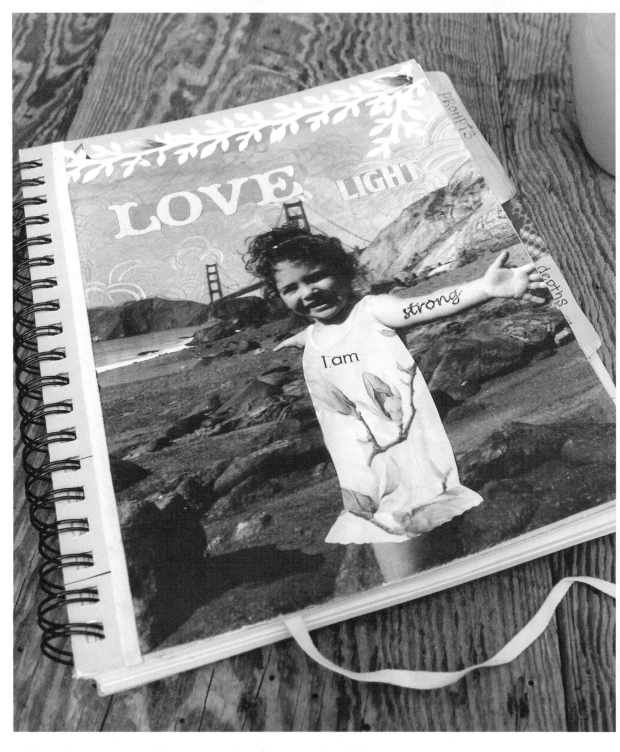

Open-Heart Journal

(I am strong)

This hand-bound notebook will hold your thoughts and dreams safely during vulnerable times. This journal acts as both a container and a record of the transformative work occuring as you move through your process of healing. Use this as you respond to the Heart Prompts offered with each project.

The cover is a sacred reminder of your core self—something often forgotten while we are swept up in the waves of change. Recall a time when you were younger, innocent, and full of joy. Many of us also have a place where we felt safe, happy, and truly at ease.

The photo on my journal cover was taken at my favorite beach, in front of the Golden Gate Bridge, when I was small. It not only demonstrates my pure joy but also depicts where I grew up. I've always loved this picture, but the inherent symbolism of the bridge in the background made it the obvious choice for my cover. To me it represents my ability to connect that small self to who I would ultimately become. Somewhere in your collection of photos, you may also stumble upon a picture that ties together the many stories you've lived so far—whether it be of you, a specific place, or an image that simply triggers a feeling of what you believe is the essence of who you are.

Gather words and images that epitomize where you hope your healing will take you: peace, growth, strength, acceptance, serenity, compassion, wisdom, ease, and on. Find them in magazines and books or print them from a computer.

HEART PROMPT

Our lives are our stories, and the pain that we experience is simply chapters within our journey. What word or title would you give the current chapter you are moving through and why?

MATERIALS

- **Spiral-bound mixed-media notebook (7 × 10 inches is a nice size)**
- **Black-and-white photocopy of photograph, enlarged to 8 × 10 inches if possible**
- **Colored pencils**
- **Foam brush**
- **Glue**
- **Spoon**
- **Collage images and words cut from magazines or books**
- **Scissors**
- **Ribbon**
- **Matte, clear-drying glue**
- **Old manila folders**
- **Paint**
- **Rubber stamps**
- **Stamp pad**
- **Paper cutter or craft knife and straightedge, for straight cuts**

MAKE

1. Begin with your cover. Enhance the photocopy of your photograph with colored pencils as an act of bringing to life your image or memory.

2. Using a foam brush, paint a thin layer of glue evenly over the entire back of the photograph and then adhere it to the cover. Smooth out any bumps with the underside of a spoon. Allow it to dry overnight.

3. Build a collage around that central image: Arrange words and pictures cut from magazines or books until they feel just right, and decorate the collage with ribbons.

4. Glue each piece in place.

5. Seal the entire collage by painting over it with a matte, clear-drying glue.

6. Create dividers for different sections of the journal according to how you'd like to organize it (I divided mine into three sections: prompts, notes, and quotes/poetry): cut old manila folders to fit over interior pages of the journal, incorporating the tab.

7. Paint the back side of the cut folder with glue and adhere it to a page.

8. Decorate the dividers with collage, paint, stamps, or all of them. Label the tabs for easy referencing.

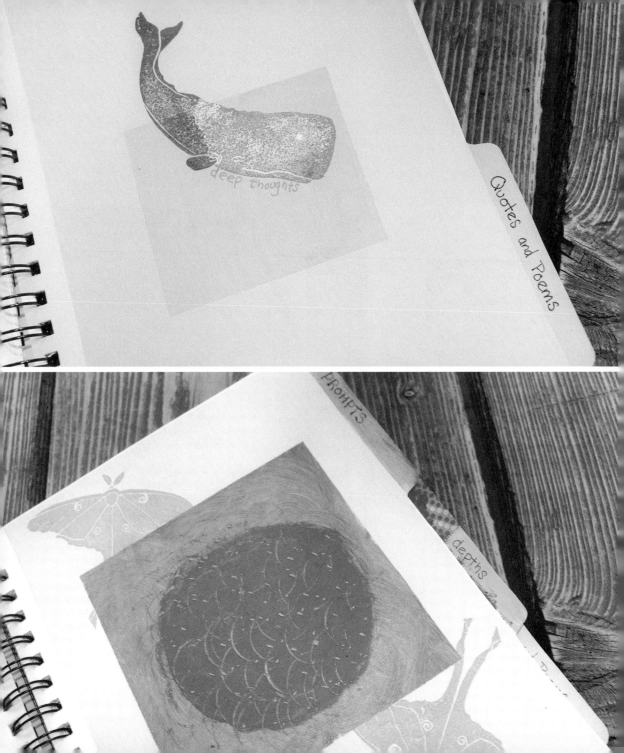

Inner Altar

(I am sacred)

When we are in the eye of the storm, it's hard to see the horizon and the blue skies ahead. An altar acts as a compass and spiritual center in your home. It's a visual reminder to be present to your life and the challenges moving through it while gently coaxing your soul forward. Friends and family may try to support us with loving words and wisdom from their own losses, but ultimately we need to find our own way back into the sun. Creating a focus point can help immensely. The process of gathering symbols and inspiration is an act of faith in yourself and a commitment to hope. If you have lost someone close to you, a second altar created just about that person and your memories of your time together is a comforting and intimate way to honor and connect with the person after he or she has passed.

This project is for making an altar for your space, but an easy variation would be to make a portable altar in an empty candy or mint tin. Cover it with paint and collage it with paper and decorative tape. Fill this tin with bits of gathered inspiration to pull out whenever needed wherever you are. You can also cover old magnets with inspiring words and store them in the tin to place on the lid when opened.

HEART PROMPT

Think of a place where you feel safe, loved, inspired. What colors and images are you drawn to over and over again? Why? Is there a word that feels especially powerful for you right now? Why? Use these locations, colors, and words as focal points in your assemblage.

- **Paintbrush**
- **Wooden crate (clementine boxes work well)**
- **Paint**
- **Glue**
- **Patterned paper**
- **Images from magazines**
- **Ephemera**
- **Words cut from periodicals or printed from the computer**
- **Photographs**
- **Small nails or tacks**
- **Jute twine or wire, for hanging**

1. Using a paintbrush, cover each side of the crate with paints and/or glue on patterned paper in a palette that sooths and inspires you.

2. Gather images and ephemera such as small tokens from nature or found objects that represent peace and growth in the direction that's most meaningful for you.

3. Add your gathered materials, along with your words and photographs, to the interior (sides) of your crate using glue and even small nails or tacks if necessary. Keep the base/floor of the box free and clear to spotlight different treasures that call out to you at any given moment.

4. Add wire or a string loop to the back of the crate. Simply insert a tack securely into the thickest part of the wood on either side of the back. Knot a length of jute or wire from one tack to the other, to hang the altar on the wall.

Lights for the End of the Tunnel

(I am shining)

The spiritual act of lighting candles has been a part of countless cultures and religions throughout history. There are a myriad of reasons one might seek the comfort and inspiration of a flame. Whether in community or in solitude, we light candles as an offering of prayer or gratitude or as a tradition or ritual. Making our own little lights is a sacred act of hope. The simple method described below is both fulfilling and easy. Give your candle extra meaning by printing a wish on the holder to seal your intention each time you light it.

> **HEART PROMPT**
>
> When times are tough, calling upon our personal beacons is another way of seeking light. What or who shines brightly when you're struggling?

1. Make a snake out of a fist-sized chunk of air-dry clay.

2. Place the clay snake on a sheet of parchment paper and use a rolling pin to flatten it into a long, thin rectangle about ½ inch thick.

3. Cut your rectangle of clay to fit around the outside of the can: Using a measuring tape, measure the height of the can and the length of the perimeter (around the can). These two numbers will be the width (the can height) and the length (the can perimeter) of your clay rectangle. Cut the clay to size by placing a straightedge or a ruler directly on top and slicing away excess clay with a knife. Wrap the clay around the outside of the can and join the ends of the clay with your fingers, gently smoothing the crease.

4. Practice printing stamps onto an extra piece of clay to get a sense of how deep you want to push in each letter. Then stamp a word directly on the clay that's wrapped around the can while the clay is still soft.

5. Let the clay dry for 24 hours, after which you can paint it if desired.

6. Melt the beeswax in an old pot.

7. Tie one end of the wick to the pencil. Cut the other end so that the length from the pencil is equal to the can's height.

8. Center the wick over the can with the pencil balanced across the top of the can and pour the hot wax into the can. Allow the wax to cool before snipping or untying the wick from the pencil.

Light your candle in ceremony or simply to bring comfort and light during the darkest times.

- **Air-dry clay**
- **Parchment paper**
- **Rolling pin or glass bottle**
- **Empty and clean shallow tin can (such as a tuna can)**
- **Measuring tape**
- **Ruler or straightedge**
- **Plastic knife**
- **Alphabet stamps or a word stamp**
- **Acrylic paint and paintbrush (optional)**
- **Beeswax or old beeswax candle stubs (quantity needed will vary depending on your can size—fill can with chunks and stubs to overflowing for a rough estimate, as the wax will take up less space when melted)**
- **Old pot for melting wax**
- **Wick (I find wicks in the candle-making sections of craft stores.)**
- **Pencil**

Breathe Cuff

(I am mindful)

Sometimes a pause and a deep breath are all we need to recalibrate. This wristband is a cuff with superpowers. Wear it during times of stress and you'll have the perfect dose of aromatherapy at your fingertips, literally. Lavender has an amazing ability to calm your senses and offers just the right dose of peace when you've been momentarily derailed. The reminder to breathe, in conjunction with a slow inhale of the soothing fragrance, will bring you right back to your center.

HEART PROMPT

Think of the place that brings you instant serenity. Is it somewhere you can visit easily or is it only part of a memory? Either way, close your eyes and imagine what it feels like to be there—the sounds, the quality of light, the temperature of the air on your skin. Fully envision this tranquil oasis and practice visiting it with each inhale of lavender.

- **Small letter stamps**
- **Ink pad (for textiles)**
- **Scraps of light-colored linen**
- **2 pieces lightweight fabric measuring 7 × 2½ inches**
- **Scissors**
- **Needle and thread or sewing machine**
- **Iron and ironing board**
- **1–2 teaspoons dried lavender**
- **2–3 inches elastic**
- **Pins**

STEP 2

Lavender

STEP 4

STEP 6-7

1. Using the letter stamps, print a reminder word (such as *breathe, be, slow, embrace, truth,* or the like) on a scrap piece of light-colored linen. I used a ruler to keep it somewhat neat, but a slightly skewed letter or two adds to the hand-stamped soul of it. Trim this scrap into a rectangle.

2. Center your printed word on the right side of one of the lightweight-fabric rectangles and sew it in place. The fabric edges around the word will be raw.

3. Lay the rectangles together, right side to right side, and sew along the two long sides about ½ inch from the edge. Turn the fabric right side out to reveal a tube. Press the tube with an iron.

4. Create the center sachet by sewing across the flattened tube, from the top to the bottom, directly over one of the side seams holding down your word. (A decorative stitch was used for the Breathe Cuff shown.) Fill the sachet with the lavender—you don't need a lot.

5. Sew up the other side of the sachet following the other seam on the opposite side of your word.

6. Fold the open ends of the cuff inward about ½ inch and press with an iron. Insert ½ inch of one end of the elastic into one of the open ends of the cuff. Pin it in place and stitch the opening closed.

7. Repeat for the other side, but before sewing, adjust the elastic to make sure the cuff sits comfortably on your wrist while still easily sliding on and off. Pin the elastic in place and stitch the opening closed.

Breathe in. And out. Find your peace.

Rest-Easy Spray

(I am peaceful)

In the first few months after my separation, sleep eluded me. My children were also frequently restless at night. A specially made spray by Anna Wingfield was a lifesaver. She created this new blend just for you; this updated recipe will not only help you sleep but also calm you during times of distress.

This spray uses lavender (for balance), rose geranium (to nurture and soothe the central nervous system), and chamomile (to relax the mind and body). The addition of flower essences adds even more power from the earth. One of Anna's favorite things about essential oils is their ability to balance and nurture us alongside life's ups and downs— this spray is a testament to their ability to do just that. Make a bottle for your bedside and one for on the go.

HEART PROMPT

Sleep and rest are essential to happy and productive days. In addition to spritzing pillows with this potion, what habits can you change to ensure a more restful night? Here are some suggestions to consider: drink less coffee, take a hot bath, eliminate screen time a few hours before bedtime, practice meditation in the evening to quiet your mind.

MATERIALS

- 10 drops lavender essential oil
- 5 drops chamomile essential oil
- 5 drops rose geranium essential oil
- 1–2 drops valerian flower essence
- 2-ounce glass bottle (I like a Boston round style in amber or cobalt blue)
- Dropper
- Distilled water
- Atomizer
- Sticker, ribbon, or dried flowers to decorate bottle (optional)

MAKE

1. Add all of the essential oils and the flower essence to the bottle with a dropper. Fill the bottle with the distilled water to about ½ inch below where the shoulder of the bottle goes into the neck, screw on the atomizer, shake, and spritz.
2. Decorate and label the bottle with stickers, a ribbon, or dried flowers if desired.

Use this spray to relax before sleep or at any time when you wish there were a volume control on life. May you find your peace.

Nourish: Rooted Stew

This recipe is not only delicious but restorative. Humble root vegetables are featured for their ability to nourish and ground us. A steaming bowl literally roots you to your body. Try eating with chopsticks and take one bite of vegetables before drinking the savory broth. It's a mini-meditation in a bowl. Keeping a pot of Rooted Stew in the fridge ensures a balancing meal just when you need it most.

An assortment of roots is used in this stew, and I would encourage you to experiment with some that may be new to you. Burdock, especially, has a long history in Asian and Native American cultures both in cuisine and for medicinal purposes. Its robust, earthy flavor adds a healing quality to each bite.

INGREDIENTS

- 1 onion, diced
- 2 cloves garlic, minced
- 1–2 tablespoons olive oil
- 5 cups assorted root vegetables, scrubbed and chopped, such as burdock, carrot, daikon, rutabaga, parsnip, turnip, celeriac
- 7 cups water
- 4–6 shiitake mushrooms, sliced, with stems removed
- 1 tablespoon fresh ginger, chopped or grated (more to taste if you're a ginger lover)
- 1 piece kombu (sea vegetable)
- ½ cup tamari
- ½ cup kudzu flakes or cornstarch, for thickening
- Rice, for serving (optional)
- Fresh scallions, sliced, for serving

MAKE

1. Sauté the onion and garlic in the olive oil for several minutes.
2. Add all of the chopped root vegetables. Pour in the water and bring to a boil. Lower the heat and add the shitake, ginger, kombu, and tamari. Simmer until the vegetables are just tender—around 40 minutes.
3. Add the cornstarch or kudzu to ½ cup cool water. Whisk. Add this mixture to the pot and keep cooking until the stew thickens.
4. Serve with rice or alone in a deep bowl. Top with scallions. Relax.

SYNCHRONICITY

You are a child of the universe, no less than the trees and the stars; you have a right to be here. And whether or not it is clear to you, no doubt the universe is unfolding as it should.

—MAX EHRMANN, *Desiderata*

I HAVE BEEN PROFOUNDLY TOUCHED by how the natural world has consistently provided clear signposts to illuminate my path. It's in the moments I've felt utterly lost that I have discovered how connected we are—to each other and to the universe. It's as if the leaves and trees, the birds and sky are all witness to our pain and our joy. Appreciating how life's lessons and rhythms are mirrored in plants, animals, and even the weather can help us to make sense out of confusion and feel less alone. There is a current that flows between everything, but it's perceptible only if we are willing and ready to recognize it.

My first experience with this feeling was on a Mother's Day a number of years ago. The January prior, on a frozen morning long before the sun had risen, I miscarried in my second trimester. Hemorrhaging began instantly, and our icy country road was nearly impossible for the ambulance to navigate. I lost what would have been our second child, and my own life came dangerously close to ending. Trauma made way for grief as I staggered through the rest of the winter, brokenhearted. When spring rolled in, I began planning a memory garden. I thought it would be a welcome ritual for the whole family and decided on a spot outside the playroom.

Before the soil was warm enough to plant, I was given a gift. It was Mother's Day, and my best friend called to send me a little extra love on this day that had me thinking of the newborn I had hoped would be in my arms that day. I was in the playroom with the phone in my hand and my eyes lingering on the spot outside the window where the garden would grow. A few random tulips currently bloomed there, and in the center was an unfamiliar and compact clump of little blue flowers. I had never planted anything in that spot before, and I not only didn't know how they had gotten there but also had no clue what they were. Luckily, my friend on the line was an avid gardener. I described the tiny star-like blossoms, and she told me that they sounded like forget-me-nots, which like to grow wild and reseed themselves in shady spots. I got goose bumps, and my heart beat faster. Forget-me-nots, indeed. It was the most memorable Mother's Day present I've ever received, a bouquet from the earth. In that moment of revelation, the broken parts inside me began their slow process of mending.

Loss and trauma can be catalysts for opening our eyes to the invisible web we are all linked to. Perhaps it's because life's biggest storms forever change us; the lens through which we view the world shifts to accommodate this reordered landscape, with all of our other senses following suit. It's in this state of heightened awareness that synchronicity shows itself most clearly.

We've all experienced a coincidence that felt almost too remarkable to believe. It's as if a message or sign arrived just when we needed it most, much like those forget-me-nots appeared to me. Carl Jung described this kind of synchronicity as a link between two events that are connected through their meaning but cannot be explained through cause and effect.

When we are broken open, the human response is to ask: Why? How could this have happened? We search desperately for answers, but often the reasons are beyond our understanding. By staying tuned in, we keep the door open for insight in unexpected places. An experience that links us to something bigger, whatever our belief system is, can help us find solace and comfort.

Acknowledging the significance during one of these occurrences is key to experiencing its therapeutic gifts. Synchronicities have the ability to spark healing because they deliver a taste of the extraordinary. The signs they provide may even cause a skeptic to pause and wonder at the mystery of it all.

When my husband left, I experienced another synchronistic phenomenon. One day, three boxes of my newly published first book arrived on my front porch—several days earlier I had stood in the same spot as those neatly stacked boxes bracing myself as I watched my husband of sixteen years drive away, never to live in our home again. I had just achieved a lifelong goal, to write a book, and yet celebrating was the last thing I felt like doing. Devastated and utterly confused, I wondered how the world could have turned upside down so suddenly. Worries about how I would care for my children and what the future held were at the forefront of my mind. Right on cue the school bus pulled up, and I rearranged my face to give my children what they needed most: my stability. My kids ran up the driveway, and then they saw what was lined up next to me. "Is it the book?" they shouted excitedly. Their enthusiasm was infectious, and I handed them each a copy to check out. It was a beautiful spring afternoon, so we headed to the picnic table out back. They sat in the sun searching for the photographs of themselves, laughing and joking with each other. I don't know if it was because of the joyful scene in front of me, but I suddenly felt calm. A clear sense that we would all be fine rose up from my toes, and as the smile spread across my face, my son looked up at me, and then above me. His mouth dropped open and he pointed straight up. We all stared at the unusual rainbow floating in the cloudless blue sky. There was something captivating about it—it was upside down. Turn a rainbow over, and do you know what it looks like? A giant, colorful smile! A grinning rainbow is a beautiful sight at any time, but in that moment the universe was beaming directly down on my little family. And I knew for certain that we'd be all right.

I encourage you to welcome symbols and signs that show up in unexpected ways to nurture a sense of connection. Keep your mind and heart open with the projects that follow. The Mandala Mirror offers new perceptions in our self-reflection, and the Nest and Egg invite the use of intuition to see what's ahead. The Wise Cap keeps us in touch with how much we already know, while the Dream Mobile protects us at night and the Blank Canvas fosters a sense of limitless potential.

SYNCHRONICITY: A GUIDED MEDITATION

Before taking on each of the following projects, consider reserving ten to fifteen minutes for an intentional pause. Crisis and transitions can bring our senses into a state of overload. Slowing down to listen, smell, taste, and feel all that is happening in one moment makes room for the integration of it all.

With gentle attention, sit comfortably yet upright. With intention, take several deep breaths and then allow your breath to be natural. See what it is like to relax as much as possible. Soften at the eyes. Try on a smile at the eyes and the mouth, reverberating down to the heart. A smile, even a slight upturn at the mouth, gives our nervous system an invitation to relax.

Chest open, belly soft, let your awareness return, again and again, to the sensations of your breath—the inflow and outflow. Let this breath be a kind of home base, a gateway to being here.

Whenever you notice that your thoughts have wandered to the past or future, that is a moment of awareness—a homecoming. If it helps, consider placing your hand on your heart as a loving reminder that you can be home in any moment.

Loss, unexpected change, or difficult transitions can offer opportunities for a kind of transformation we never thought possible. When we are in the middle of a storm, anything can happen. A shift, ever so slight, and our life takes a turn. When we get very still in the center of something swirling, we may be able to take hold of slender threads—a chance meeting, an intuitive knowing, an unexpected moment, a subtle message in the wind. Welcome the gifts when a storm blows in; they will not be predictable or expected. In fact, they appear in many forms, but have faith that they arrive to lead us forward—allowing our lives to unfold. Listen. Watch. And welcome.

Mandala Mirror

(I am whole)

Seeing yourself clearly is challenging even during stress-free times. The Mandala Mirror encourages you to look beyond the surface with a reminder of who you truly are. It also invites you to set intentions for qualities you'd like to cultivate. Position this mirror where everyday glances are sure to happen and rotate the mandala messages to suit your needs. A mandala is a circular symbol in Hindu and Buddhism that represents the universe, wholeness, and infinity. The act of making small ones is a wonderful form of meditation without any art skills necessary.

HEART PROMPT

When you look in the mirror, what do you see? Do you recognize within yourself the qualities and traits that you admire most in others? How can you bring the essence of them into your core being?

MAKE

1. Gather your materials for painting and take them to a comfortable spot by a window, or even better, take them outside.
2. Remind yourself that you are calming the mind, not creating a masterpiece.
3. Beginning with the pen, draw a small circle in the center of the watercolor paper. Add four matching shapes (triangles, flower petals) to the perimeter of the circle—one for each direction.
4. Continue adding shapes and doodles evenly around the circle.
5. Fill in the design with watercolors. There is no rush. Find your rhythm. Breathe.
6. Make as many little mandalas as you like. Title each with an attribute that you'd like to see in yourself when you gaze upon your reflection.
7. Punch a hole at the top center of each square.
8. Gently hammer a nail into the top corners of the mirror's frame.
9. If you like, decorate the nail by coating it lightly with glue and wrapping embroidery thread around it up to the nail head.
10. Hang your mandala paintings and even special jewelry, such as the Breathe Cuff or Nautical Necklace, from the nails.

MATERIALS

- **Fine-point waterproof black pen (Micron brand pens work well)**
- **Watercolor paper cut into 3- × 3-inch squares**
- **Watercolors and fine brushes**
- **Jar of water for watercolors**
- **Hole punch**
- **Hammer**
- **Small nails**
- **Mirror with wooden frame**
- **Glue**
- **Embroidery thread (optional)**

Nest and Egg

(*I am intuitive*)

We all hold the answers within. Trusting this and accessing them are the challenge. This project embraces that idea by having you create an empty painted egg that holds a special message to your future self. Cradle it in a nest made of words lovingly scripted to who you feel you will be in one year's time. What a tender gift and how lovely it looks waiting for you—reminding you that you do know. You do.

HEART PROMPT

When you think back to a younger version of yourself, what message would you want to give to her? Is there some wisdom you might offer her from your present experience?

MATERIALS

- **Egg**
- **Pin**
- **Drinking straw**
- **Letter to self in one year**
- **Brief message on tiny strip of paper (to be rolled up tightly to fit in the hole in the egg)**
- **Black tea, steeped well**
- **Scissors**
- **Thread, yarn, or string**
- **Teacup or small bowl**
- **Plastic wrap**
- **White glue**
- **Foam brushes**
- **Tissue paper or old sewing-pattern paper**
- **Acrylic paints**

MAKE

1. Blow out the contents of the egg (whites and yolk) by tapping a hole into the bottom and top of it with the pin. Place the straw over the top hole and blow steadily through it until the liquid of the egg starts pouring out the bottom hole. (Catch it in a bowl for scrambled eggs in the morning.) Blowing out the egg enlarges the bottom hole.

2. Rinse the egg, inside and out, and let it dry for several days.

3. Meanwhile, write a love letter to your older self. Put some thought into who your future self might be. Think of who and what you'll be in ten years, and then work backward to five years from now. How about one year? Who will you have become? Where will you have journeyed? Compose a love letter to yourself to read one year from now. Be generous and effusive with your affection and compassion.

4. In addition to the letter, write a brief message or short excerpt on a tiny slip of paper. Roll up the message and set it aside for when it's time to fill the egg.

5. To make the nest, begin by painting the letter to yourself with black tea to create an aged look. Allow it to dry.

6. Cut the letter into skinny strips the width of the paper. Add thread, string, or yarn to the tangle of paper and shape it into a nest with your hands.

7. Line the inside of a bowl or cup with plastic wrap. Dilute the glue with a few drops of water and use a foam brush to paint this mixture on the plastic wrap all around the inside of the bowl.

8. Insert the paper nest and fine-tune the nest shape, making sure the open part of the nest is large enough to hold the egg. Add some of the water/glue solution to the nest until it is damp but not soggy. Set it outside in the sun or in a bright window to dry.
9. Remove the nest from the bowl once it has dried and hardened and peel off the plastic wrap.
10. Return to the egg: Insert the small, rolled-up message into one of the egg's holes. Cover the egg in a diluted water/glue mixture and layer on scraps of tissue paper until the egg is covered, including both holes.
11. Once the glue has dried, paint the egg with acrylics. Place the egg in the nest and display them on your altar or another special place. Don't open your egg for a year. Mark your calendar for when it's time to crack it open.

Dream Mobile

(I am protected)

A dream catcher's job is to ensnare bad dreams in the web and let the positive ones slip through the center opening. Those good dreams travel down the feathers to the sleeping person below. Many Native American tribes traditionally created dream catchers to protect sleep time. If your nights are haunted with shadows, you may rest more deeply with this Dream Mobile above your bed. This particular dream catcher is suspended like a mobile to let the feathers dance in even the slightest movement of air—it captivates during the day but does its job when the sun goes down.

> **HEART PROMPT**
>
> As you gather your materials, visualize throwing a net around your demons to capture them and keep them from visiting you during your precious hours of sleep needed for recharging for the next day.

MATERIALS

- **Inner hoop of an embroidery frame (must be larger than the doily)**
- **1-inch-wide strips of lightweight fabric (a bed sheet or muslin works well)**
- **Needle**
- **Embroidery floss, button thread, or other strong thread**
- **Circular doily or scrap of lace**
- **Scissors**
- **Feathers (real or paper ones made from template on pages 122–23)**
- **Beads, semiprecious stones, charms, talismans, or other such items**
- **Watercolors and paintbrush (optional)**

MAKE

1. Wrap the hoop in fabric: Place the end of one of the fabric strips on the inside of the hoop and wrap the fabric around the hoop in evenly spaced overlapping edges until the entire hoop is covered and no longer visible. Add more strips by incorporating them from the inside of the hoop. When finished, secure the end of the strip to the inside of the hoop with a needle and thread and several stitches.

2. Attach the doily or lace to the hoop with thread: Tie and knot sections of the doily to the hoop, beginning at the twelve o'clock and six o'clock positions. Pull the doily taut. Then move on to the three o'clock and nine o'clock sections. Work your way around until the entire doily is secure and evenly distributed.

3. Cut two pieces of thread that are each twice the length of the diameter of the hoop. With what will be the back of the hoop facing up, tie the ends of one thread to the twelve o'clock and six o'clock positions. Tie the ends of the other thread at the three o'clock and nine o'clock positions of the hoop. Tie the two threads together at the apex with a third strand of thread. This piece should be long enough to suspend the hoop from the ceiling. This third thread will need a loop at the end.

4. Dangle feathers, beads, and so on from the doily or hoop on different lengths of thread. Paper feathers can be printed on card stock. Use as is, or paint over the feathers with a wash of watercolors.

Wise Cap

(I am insightful)

Some days walking out the front door can be more of a challenge than others. The security of a good hat can go a long way in promoting your confidence and helping you feel pulled together. This little beret does all of that and more, with a hidden message stitched inside the band. Never doubt your wisdom or insights again. This sweet hat is your secret weapon—you are a force to be reckoned with.

HEART PROMPT

What message would you like whispered each time you don your cap? Think about favorite quotes, your grandmother's sayings, and lines of poetry.

- **Tailor's chalk or pencil**
- **12-inch circle template (see Creating a Circle Template on page 115)**
- **½ yard each of wool (exterior) and linen (lining) fabric (this is the perfect way to recycle some well-loved clothing)**
- **Scissors**
- **Pins**
- **Needle and button thread or sewing machine**
- **Small rectangle of light-colored jersey from a T-shirt**
- **Fabric marker**

1. Trace the circle template twice on the wool fabric for the exterior and twice on the linen for the lining. Cut them all out for a total of four 12-inch circles.

2. Cut a 6- to 6½-inch circle from the center of one exterior circle and one lining circle. Discard the cut-out circle; the remaining donut shape is where your head will go. Start out small and try it on for size—you can always adjust it to make it bigger. It should slip over your head easily.

3. Cut a long band 1½ inches wide from both the exterior and lining fabrics. Determine the length by measuring around your head (where the hat will sit), then add ½ inch.

4. Place the exterior circle and exterior donut together, right side to right side. Pin and sew the two circles together around the outer edge. As the seam allowance isn't terribly important, use the presser foot of your sewing machine (if you're using one) as a guide. If sewing by hand, use a seam allowance of ½ inch. Sew completely around the circle, as shown.

5. Sew the 1½-inch ends of the exterior band together, right side to right side, using a ½ inch seam allowance.

6. Insert the exterior band into the exterior donut, aligning the cut edges with right side to right side. Pin in place and then sew the pieces together using the pressure foot as your seam-allowance gauge.

7. Repeat steps 4 through 6 with the lining fabric.

8. Write your quote or saying on the piece of jersey fabric with the fabric marker. Cut it out to fit inside the

STEP 2

STEP 4

width of the band. Center it over the seam on the right side of the lining band and stitch it in place.

9. Turn the exterior fabric right side out and insert it into the lining (not turned yet) so that the lining and exterior have right sides together. Pin the bands together.

10. Sew around the entire band, leaving a 3-inch hole for turning.

11. Pull the hat right side out through the hole and tuck the lining into place.

12. Tuck in the edges of the turning hole and press the entire band with an iron. Sew the hole closed with small stitches or edge stitch around the entire hatband on the sewing machine.

Blank Canvas

(I am filled with possibility)

Sleep is essential. We spend many hours of each day trying to get enough, so why not utilize that time with some inspiration above our head or across from our bed for the moment when we wake up. No prior painting experience is necessary to create a huge work of art. A big blank canvas holds the profound message that we are always evolving and have choices. When we've just been broken open and are searching for answers and meaning, a large visual reminder of this is a welcome tool. Adding a single color to the canvas maintains the sense of unlimited potential while providing mood enhancement evoked by the specific color selected. There is also a sense of freedom in knowing that you can just paint over the canvas with a different color as your needs change.

HEART PROMPT

How do you feel most of the time right now? What would you like to change? Which color would help you most to get there?

- **Drop cloth**
- **Large stretched canvas**
- **Acrylic paint (house paint works well for a large surface)**
- **Paintbrush**

1. Choose a color that speaks to where you are right now. Use the list of colors and their meanings here to help you.
2. Set aside a block of time that will be uninterrupted. Make some tea or pour yourself a glass of wine. Play music. Light a candle.
3. Spread out your drop cloth on the floor or on a large table. Arrange the canvas, paint, and brush on top.
4. Paint! Fill the canvas. There is no right or wrong way. Run your fingers through the paint if you like. Cover the canvas uniformly or allow the original canvas to show through in places. Enjoy immersing yourself in a color that fills you up.

COLORS AND THEIR CORRESPONDING MEANINGS

Red. Represents strength, power, determination, as well as passion, desire, and love.

Orange. Combines the energy of red and the happiness of yellow. It's associated with enthusiasm, fascination, happiness, creativity; and it symbolizes encouragement and success.

Yellow. The color of sunshine. It's associated with joy, happiness, intellect, and energy.

Green. Has great healing power. It is considered the most restful color for our eyes. Green suggests growth, harmony, freshness, and fertility.

Blue. The color of the sky and sea, often associated with depth and stability. It symbolizes trust, loyalty, wisdom, confidence, intelligence, faith, and heaven. Blue is considered beneficial to the mind and body. It slows our metabolism and produces a calming state of mind.

Purple. Combines the stability of blue and the energy of red. Purple is associated with royalty, power, nobility, luxury, and ambition. It is associated with wisdom, dignity, independence, creativity, mystery, and magic.

White. Associated with light, good, innocence, and purity. It is considered the color of perfection.

Nourish: Spicy Sisters Stew

Chunks of sweet butternut squash and kernels of corn mingle with savory black beans in a thick broth that has hints of smoky chipotle chilies. Besides being delicious, this stew meets my three biggest criteria for family recipes: it packs a powerful nutritional punch, it's fairly quick to throw together, and it satisfies all of our dietary preferences and sensitivities. We enjoy this with brown rice or quinoa and a nice side of greens. Leftovers are delicious and satisfying when put in a cast-iron skillet, topped with cornbread batter, and baked in the oven until golden.

This stew was named after the Three Sisters: corn, beans, and squash. Various Native American tribes grew them as companion plants and referred to them as the sisters.

INGREDIENTS

- 1 onion, chopped
- Several cloves of garlic, minced
- 2 tablespoons olive oil
- 1 medium butternut squash, peeled and cubed
- Approximately 4 cups water or vegetable stock
- 3 cups cooked or 2 cans black beans (leftovers are perfect used here)
- 1 cup corn kernels (fresh or frozen)
- 2 tomatoes, chopped (optional)

- Salt and pepper
- Dried oregano to taste
- Dash of cumin
- ½ teaspoon adobo sauce to taste

OPTIONS FOR SERVING

- Fresh cilantro
- Chipotle chilies in adobo sauce
- Crème fraîche or thick yogurt
- Chopped tomatoes
- Freshly grated cheddar cheese or a soft goat cheese
- Brown rice or quinoa

1. Sauté the onions and garlic in the olive oil in a heavy-bottomed pot for 5 minutes. Add the squash and just enough of the water or vegetable stock to cover the squash. Simmer for 15 minutes.
2. Add the beans, corn, and tomatoes. Then pour in the remaining 2 cups of water or vegetable stock. Add more or less liquid depending on how thick you'd like this stew. Stir in the salt, pepper, oregano, cumin, and adobo sauce.
3. Simmer until the squash is tender and the flavors have melded. Cook for at least 20 minutes more if you need to get dinner on the table soon or cook for longer to enhance the flavors of the stew.
4. Set the table with bowls of any or all of the serving options at the ready for your diners.

HEALING

It has been said, "time heals all wounds."
I do not agree. The wounds remain. In
time, the mind, protecting its sanity, cov-
ers them with scar tissue and the pain
lessens. But it is never gone.

—ROSE KENNEDY

THE ACT OF HEALING will look different for each of us. There is no need to rush—nor a clear timetable for traveling through the unique terrain of each loss. Death of a loved one, a traumatic life event, or deep heartbreak are all wounds that have the potential never to leave us. The scars remain to remind us of what we've felt, whom we've loved, and how we've grown. They become part of the fabric of our lives.

I sew. A lot. The metaphors that surround needle and thread seep into my thoughts often. The British proverb "A stitch in time saves nine" is a favorite. The meaning is simple: sew up a little hole with one stitch now so that it doesn't expand and turn into something greater that may need nine or more stitches. It's a saying that refers to doing things well the first time and not putting something off until later. Healing well from the start is an unhurried and deliberate mending. The frayed and broken fibers of our stories can almost always be woven back together, but how we choose to repair and patch ourselves up determines quite a bit. A quick fix is sure to leave you weak for unraveling. This is true in the literal sense, such as stitching up a hole in a seam. Why wouldn't it also be true for our souls?

I believe that taking supremely good care of yourself will strengthen every muscle—including your heart. You'll be ready for that moment when the dark clouds begin to part. Think of self-care as an umbrella during the storm. It offers some protection even if it's pouring. You might still get soaked but maybe not as much. And when the sun breaks through, and it always does, that umbrella remains—perhaps thrown back so you can feel the warmth spreading across your smiling face, but always available as your shelter from the many seasons of life.

My experience with diet and grief surprised me but also jump-started a self-care program that grew into the guidelines that follow. I've always loved food. I enjoy reading about it, preparing it, serving it, and most of all eating it. In addition, when

I need some form of comfort or feel empty in any way, it's what I've always reached for. Obviously, I am not alone—thousands of books and websites are devoted to the relationship we have with food. However, a strange and common phenomenon happens when we experience sudden trauma. It's an instant appetite suppressant for many, even some of us comfort eaters. It can be extreme and alarming. Nothing had ever made me literally *forget* to eat until my husband left. Food became meaningless. I'd reach the end of the day and realize that two mealtimes had disappeared without my noticing. Of course, I still diligently cooked and baked for my kids—preparing delicious food for them has always been an extension of my love. While I poured my soul into making special meals for them in the months that followed, I found myself unable to fill my body with the love I offered. I began to shrink. Normally, I would have been thrilled—but I didn't care. It didn't matter. But what was of concern was how I showed up for my children. I couldn't be weak. I couldn't get sick. It felt like the entire world rested on my shoulders, and they needed to be *strong*.

So I made a decision to eat, not for the pleasure of it, but for the power of it. This meant that everything I put into my body needed to be nutrient dense and pure. Forgetting about meals wasn't an option anymore. And so I drank a lot of green smoothies because they were easy and I didn't have to think about it. Blend it. Drink it. In those first few months alone, my blender whirred almost every day. Green smoothies saved me. My recipe for keepin' going when the going gets rough is at the end of this chapter.

I've designed a selection of projects to support you in this moment—from a clever cushion to lean on to a talisman to wear and a ritual for releasing. There is also a deck of miniretreat cards to keep self-care at your fingertips. And last, I've included an easy-to-construct life vest for staying afloat in luxurious cashmere.

SELF-CARE SUGGESTIONS

Below are the principles that I followed so that I could try to stay healthy and strong even when that was the last thing on my mind. Come up with your own list of guidelines that you can also refer to again and again.

BODY

EAT. Make a conscious effort to consume only delicious, beautiful, and nutritious food.

DRINK. Imbibe prolific amounts of water. Most of us are always a little dehydrated. You'd be surprised how powerful taking in more fluids really is. (Coffee and black tea don't count!)

MOVE. Get your blood pumping—outside when possible. This is essential. Exercise boosts your mood when it releases endorphins, eases stress, and helps you sleep.

DIG. Plant a garden or help a friend with hers. Weeding is a fantastically therapeutic way to spend time outside, and the act of clearing a space is a wonderful metaphor for opening a space for new beginnings.

MIND

READ. Find any books that pertain to your particular crisis and/or indulge in a wonderfully written novel that takes you to another time or place that you don't already know about.

LAUGH. Watch or listen to something totally funny.

LEARN. Do something new. Rewire your brain with something that you've always wanted to try or something that never even crossed your mind. It can be something small—any effort counts. A new language, knitting, cooking, skiing, painting, you name it. Online classes make this easy and nonthreatening for so many subjects these days.

SOUL

CREATE. Make something with your hands.

QUIET. Make time for silence—it allows your soul (and heart) space for mending. Schedule it into your calendar if you have to. Take a walk in nature regularly.

MEDITATE. Begin a daily practice.

YOGA. Connecting body, mind, and soul makes yoga an invaluable part of treating yourself well.

JOURNAL. The act of taking the words out of your head and putting them elsewhere for safekeeping is always freeing and extremely effective.

RELEASE. Let go of patterns and things that you don't need. Declutter your mind and home.

Acknowledge how important it is to make time for restoration. Slowing down will enhance each project offered in this chapter. Set aside ten to fifteen minutes to find stillness and be mindful, any time of day or just before you begin your creative process.

With gentle attention, sit comfortably yet upright. With intention, take several deep breaths and then allow your breath to be natural. See what it is like to relax as much as possible. Soften at the eyes. Try on a smile at the eyes and the mouth, reverberating down to the heart. A smile, even a slight upturn at the mouth, gives our nervous system an invitation to relax.

Chest open, belly soft, let your awareness return again and again to the sensations of your breath—the inflow and outflow. Let this breath be a kind of home base.

Whenever you notice that your thoughts have wandered to past or future, that is a moment of awareness—a homecoming. Place your hand on your heart as a loving reminder that you can be home in any moment. Breathe into your healing heart.

Listen for your deepest and most sincere intention. What is it that matters to you? What is it you want to touch, realize, discover, and trust?

The act of homecoming is arriving, moment after moment, at the alive interplay of sounds, sensations, emotion, thoughts within us—and greeting all of it with warmth and friendliness. You might ask yourself: Is there anything between me and being "home" in this moment? Often there is much in the way. Past experiences have told us not to rely on our knowing, yet healing happens when we grapple with the messy practice of trusting our own direct lived and sensed experience. This refuge offers us a place to be with our own fears, negative emotions, narratives, and inner weather.

Our suffering occurs not just when difficult thoughts and emotions arise; it is more often the result of how we treat ourselves when they come. If that is so, then healing, we might say, is when we greet difficulty as a kind of homecoming—with warmth, kindness, and an embrace. What if we greet our own dear messy, flawed, and beautiful selves with sincere openheartedness? "Sweetheart, are you hurting?" Greet her lovingly, right now. Do not hesitate: take her into your arms, take her into your heart—in this moment . . . and in this moment . . . and in this one.

Stability Bolster

(I am supported)

A bolster is a type of firm pillow that fits perfectly behind your back or under your knees to prop you up just where you need it. Support yourself physically and emotionally when you consider what the word *bolster* is synonymous with: reinforce, boost, renew, and sustain. For this project, a distinctive piece of material artfully renews a tired and worn towel, wrapping beauty around comfort. This project requires little cutting (with a potential for zero) and no sewing. Go ahead and use your favorite aunt's beautiful scarf or that inspiring fabric you've kept tucked away for a rainy day. This cushion is so quick and clever to make that you'll want to tuck one into every cozy spot in your home.

HEART PROMPT

Self-sustaining practices are essential to fortify our health and well-being. Before you begin, or perhaps right after you've made your bolster, settle back and make a list of five things that you already do to care for yourself both physically and emotionally. Then write three more that you'd like to incorporate into your life.

- ½ yard fabric, which will work for most bath-sized towels
- Bath towel
- 2 rubber bands
- Safety pin or needle and thread (optional)

STEP 5

1. Fold over one long side of the fabric by 1 inch to the wrong side. Press with an iron to create a tidy edge.
2. Fold the towel in half lengthwise. Roll it up to create the bolster's form.
3. Spread out the fabric right side up.
4. Place the length of the rolled towel on the right side of the fabric along the edge with the pressed fold. Center the towel so that there is approximately the same amount of fabric on either end.
5. Beginning at the folded edge of the fabric, tightly roll the towel and fabric together toward the side opposite the fold. Cinch the excess fabric at each end with a rubber band to create a Tootsie Roll effect.
6. Gently remove the towel and turn the cover right side out. Insert the towel back inside and position the gathers at each end.
7. If you'd like to secure the folded edge, do so with a safety pin or a few stitches with needle and thread.

Nautical Necklace

(I am steady)

Boats were the primary form of transportation throughout much of history, and our language reflects this with an abundance of sayings and proverbs pertaining to sailing. The symbolic significance of a vessel caught in a storm or sailing on smooth seas has instant recognition, even if we've never left the shore. Navigating bad weather takes skill, and yet we often get caught under dark clouds without any preparation. We must learn as we go—to find our way and keep from capsizing. Wearing a talisman of a sailboat is a simple reminder of our ability to stay on course and ride it out. The reverse side of the necklace displays an anchor—the perfect symbol to hold on to when we feel unmoored by life's twists and turns. The weight of the washer is just enough to grasp on to and feel grounded and secure—a true anchor. My own ship and anchor images are shared in the Templates section in back of this book, but you can use any photocopy of a ship or anchor that is reduced in size to fit nicely on a washer.

HEART PROMPT

Visualize a captain searching for clear skies and smooth waters. It's physically challenging, and the fear can be overwhelming, but adjusting the sails (our thoughts) can help tremendously. No need to resist. Think of a time when you've felt like you've ridden the waves rather than met them head on. How did that feel?

- **Washer**
- **Photocopied art of sailboat and anchor (see templates on page 117)**
- **Pencil**
- **Scissors**
- **Button thread**
- **Foam brush**
- **White glue**
- **Pinch of air-dry clay or small piece of cardboard**
- **Beads (optional)**

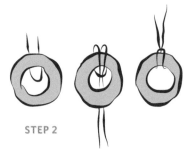

STEP 2

1. Place and center the washer over the artwork. Trace around the washer's outer circumference with a pencil. Cut out the shape with scissors. Repeat so that you have two circles of art the size of your washer.
2. Take a 30-inch length of button thread and fold it in half. Insert the fold of the thread through the center of the washer. Pass the ends of the thread through the loop that is created and pull to secure the thread.
3. With the foam brush, paint an even coat of white glue on one side of the washer and over the thread. Place one of the circles of art on top, with the thread at the center top and pulled tight. Smooth out the paper and let it dry.
4. Paint a coat of glue on top of the art to seal it. Let it dry again.
5. Take a pinch of clay, or a piece of cardboard cut to size, and press it into the center of the washer on the back side. Make it flush with the rest of the washer.
6. Repeat steps 3 and 4 using the second circle of art.
7. Add beads to the strands of thread if desired. Tie the ends of the thread together in a knot, allowing the thread to remain long enough to slip the necklace over your head.

I'm not afraid of storms, for I'm learning how to sail my ship.

—Louisa May Alcott

A smooth sea never made a skilled sailor.

—English proverb

She stood in the storm, and when the wind did not go her way, she adjusted the sails.

—Elizabeth Edwards

A ship in a harbor is safe, but that's not what ships were built for.

— John A. Shedd

Healing   67

Permission Ships

(I am letting go)

Liberate yourself from old patterns, memories, or habits with small handmade vessels created to carry your worries away. Launch them out to sea or set them on a special shelf as a reminder to let go. Many cultures around the world have customs featuring small boats filled with candles, offerings, and wishes that are sent across a body of water. India has *diya*s, small leaf boats filled with flowers and flames that are sent down the Ganges; Thailand has *krathong,* floating baskets made of bread or banana leaves; Brazil has little wooden boats sent off from the beaches of Rio on New Year's Eve to honor the ocean goddess, Lemanjá. Experience the power of letting water transport your wishes and prayers with this iteration of a powerful universal ritual.

HEART PROMPT

Before you begin, consider the obstacles that stand between you and finding peace. What are you holding on to that you'd like to release? Which words reflect what is holding you back most—such as fear or expectations—and what might freedom from them look like?

- Piece of bark or driftwood
- Cup hook
- A skewer or pointy stick
- Beeswax candle and matches
- Scissors
- Scrap of lightweight fabric or lace, for the sail
- Needle and thread
- Alphabet stamps and stamp pad
- Paper
- Glue stick

1. Make a hole for the mast (the stick) in the center of the wood; I like using a cup hook to drill the hole because it's simple and can be taken directly to the beach or lake to make boats on-site.

2. Find a stick that fits securely in the hole. Break the stick so that the height of the stick roughly matches the length of the boat.

3. Light the beeswax candle and wait until a little pool of liquid wax forms beneath the flame. Dip the bottom end of the stick into the wax. Immediately insert it into the hole in the wood and let the wax cool.

4. Cut out a right triangle of fabric for the sail. No need for perfection. Measure and adjust as you go. Attach it to the mast with needle and thread. A whipstitch works well. Alternatively, you can cut a few tiny slits in the fabric (perpendicular in direction to the mast) and weave the stick through the fabric. If you use lace, weave the mast through the holes. Small sails won't need anything more. Larger ones might need a support on the bottom edge of the sail. Use a very light, thin stick and attach it with needle and thread as used for the mast.

5. Consider what emotion you'd like to release. Stamp your releasing word or words on a piece of paper and cut it into a long skinny banner. (See suggested words opposite.) Secure the banner to the top of the mast by folding the end of the paper around the mast and gluing it to the back side of the banner.

Your boat is ready to set sail, either on display or on the nearest lake, river, or ocean. Consider sharing the experience with others. Gather with one or more close friends and make and sail boats together.

RELEASING WORD SUGGESTIONS

Grief	Habits
Struggles	Memories
Fear	Relationship patterns
Expectations	Scarcity
Pain	

Earth Care

- Spend some simple time in the garden doing seasonal chores.
- Choose one bed to focus on. Only one.
- Tend the soil as you would a child.
- Weeds can be helped out, rather than yanked.

Renewal Cards

(I am worthy)

With the help of this miniretreat deck, you'll receive some of the same benefits of a little getaway but from the comfort of your own home. Tucked inside a handmade folder are simple prompts to settle your mind, sooth your senses, and ground your spirit. Each one takes only a few moments to experience but offers a respite in the midst of everyday chaos and uncertainty. A sense of peace and focus will follow such an intentional pause in your day. Whether you need a solitary retreat or want to invite someone to join you, time spent unplugged and slowed down nourishes harmony and balance within.

These cards are especially inviting when stored in a personalized handmade folder. Try making it using only materials that you have around the house. The process of making the folder should feel inspiring—a mini–creative retreat of its own. There are several cards to print out in the Templates section and a blank for your own brainstorming. You are your own expert.

The instructions call for using Tyvek for making the folder. Tyvek is made from polyethylene fibers and commonly found in your mailbox in the form of envelopes or "mailers." It can be recycled *only* if sent back to its manufacturer, so why not reinvent it into something of use and beauty? It resembles a cross between paper and cloth but is tear- and water-resistant. Repurposing with Tyvek is always satisfying—just don't get it near a hot iron, or it will melt. If you'd rather not use Tyvek, wool is also a great option. If you choose to use wool, the folding and stitching instructions are the same; the difference is in the embellishment process. Embroidery, appliqué, or needle felting would all work beautifully on a wool folder.

HEART PROMPT

Outline several of your own personal retreats. What refreshes you? What simple act feels nourishing to your body? To your soul? To your mind?

- Scissors
- Recycled Tyvek mailer
- Craft paint, paintbrush, and rag
- Permanent markers
- Various stamps and stamp pad ink for plastic and metal
- Needle and thread or glue
- Thin strip of elastic or skinny elastic hair tie
- Small lightweight button
- Photocopy of the Renewal Cards (see pages 118–19), or make your own cards

1. Cut the Tyvek into a rectangle that measures 8½ × 11 inches.
2. Apply a generous layer of paint to what will become the interior side. Do not let it dry; instead, wipe away any excess paint with a rag to reveal the intriguing texture that the spun fibers create. Now let the paint dry.
3. Repeat step 2 on the front side. Once the paint is dry, add a drawing, decorative stamp, or words. Use permanent markers and stamp ink that is recommended for plastic and metal surfaces to ensure no smearing.
4. Place the Tyvek exterior side down and fold up the bottom edge by 3½ inches to create a pocket. Stitch the pocket in place along the left side of the folder, starting at the bottom and stitching just past the edge of the pocket. Stitch back and forth the last ½ inch for reinforcement.
5. Stitch down the whole length of the center fold, making sure to lock stitches at the beginning and end. This creates a crisp fold and secure pocket.
6. Insert both ends of the elastic into the right edge of the pocket on the right side, near the top edge of the pocket, to make a little loop fitting the size of the button that extends out to the right.

    The ends of the elastic should adjoin. This will be your button loop. Stitch the right side of the pocket just as directed in step 4, making sure that the reinforcement stitches include the elastic.
7. Sew the button to the front of the folder as close to that right side edge as possible. The elastic loop goes over the button to close the folder.
8. Fill the folder with cards.

PAUSE

Tranquility
CI 183

Sheltered Shawl

(I am cherished)

This crossover cashmere shawl is like the familiar hug of an old friend. When you're yearning for a warm embrace, button it on and you will have your own personal life vest wrapping you in softness and safety. What a tender way to proclaim your affection for yourself. The beauty of this no-sew design is that it can be completed almost instantly with a pair of scissors. The only stitching necessary is for the buttons. For the shawl fabric, use a special sweater from a loved one or search thrift stores. A very soft wool or wool blend can be substituted for cashmere. Cozy, not itchy, is the key.

HEART PROMPT

What or who makes you feel safe, cherished, and held? The act of embracing is not only a sign of affection; it's also a form of acceptance. When we embrace an experience, we are willing to look at it head-on. What parts of your current situation are you willing to accept and embrace?

- **Cashmere (or wool or wool blend) sweater**
- **Scissors**
- **2 large buttons**
- **Button thread and needle**

1. Use a sweater that fits loosely. Toss it in the washer in warm water and then the dryer to partially felt it.
2. Dissect the sweater along its seams as follows: cut off the neckline, the waistband, and the sleeves.
3. Cut straight up the side seams to open the sides completely.
4. Divide the front in half with a straight cut up the center.
5. Position the sweater over your body so that the back is in place and the two front panels swing loosely over your chest. Adjust and sparingly snip off any excess sweater until each front panel is even in length and width with the other.
6. Cross one front panel over the other, so that the corners in the front sweater panels now meet the back of the sweater along each side. Gauge where a button on each side of the back panel might be placed. Sew a button on each side of the back, spaced equally at the edges.
7. Snip a horizontal buttonhole on the inner front corner of each panel.
8. Wrap yourself in your shawl.

STEP 2

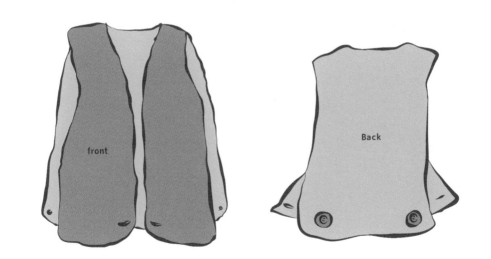

front

Back

STEP 7

Nourish: Sailing Smoothie

Packed with protein and green power, this smoothie is a meal in a glass. It's a great start to your day or the perfect boost whenever your energy is waning.

INGREDIENTS

- 1 banana
- 1 to 1½ cups water, coconut water, or juice
- 1 handful frozen fruit
- 2 teaspoons chia seeds
- Greens to fill the rest of the blender (spinach and kale are my favorites)
- 1 teaspoon spirulina (optional)
- Agave syrup or honey, to taste (optional)

MAKE

Add all of the ingredients to a blender and mix. *Be strong—eat for power!*

REINVENTION

We must let go of the life we have planned, so as to accept the one that is waiting for us.

—Joseph Campbell

I TITLED MY FIRST BOOK, *Reinvention,* long before there was even a hint that I'd be reinventing myself as it was coming off the printing press. Life's ironies are curious and inexplicable. From the beginning of time, every culture has created legends and stories to explain the mysterious and offer structure and meaning to the chaos of life. The most common myth surrounds death and resurrection or rebirth of the soul. Most of us have heard of the phoenix rising out of the ashes or the quest for the Holy Grail. Joseph Campbell, the mythology scholar, called the quest the hero's journey.

My own experience of the archetypal myth has definitely been a *reinvention.* When the unexpected arrives, this is the odyssey so many of us undertake. It is a process of falling off a cliff and embracing the painful and terrifying plummet with eyes wide open—most of the time. This dive and crash make it possible for deep transformation to occur. It is the doorway to growth. And it is how we discover our wings and remake ourselves.

When the ground slips away, the impetus to shut our eyes and hide behind our hands is strong. But pulling the covers over my head wasn't an option; children needed to be cared for and work had to be done. My public presence online kept me keenly focused on maintaining my composure. On the morning my husband announced that our marriage was over, several thousand people visited me with tea in hand for their daily dose of positivity on *maya★made,* my eco-lifestyle blog that focuses on creativity and family life. I didn't reveal what my day truly looked like. A tornado had ripped through my home, but few knew. To insulate myself from the pain, I kept the unfolding events quiet, save for the closest people in my world. As a professional shield, I continued writing my typical posts about food, crafts, and the seasons changing. *Reinvention* hit the bookshelves simultaneously, and marketing needed to be at the forefront of my mind. At night I'd lie awake alone, battling demons and longing for the morning. When the sun came up, there were school lunches to be made and dinner to go in the slow cooker. I'd link to my book tour, set up launch parties, and try desperately to keep putting one foot in front of the other. It was a surreal time of dual worlds. And it wasn't sustainable.

In this new era of social media and online connections, how we share our personal lives has come under some scrutiny. I made a very conscious decision that I would reveal some part of my story so that I could live more authentically and not feel the pressure to pretend that all was okay. I trusted that my readers would appreciate the transparency and hoped that it would help at least one person feel less alone. But choosing the right time was tricky. As months passed, it grew harder to keep up the pretense but even more challenging to find the words I wanted to share.

My annual textile class at Squam Art Workshops was on the horizon. That year I was scheduled to give a talk on the process of publishing a book. There would be close to two hundred attendees. I hadn't spoken in front of a large audience since high school and was terrified of falling apart onstage if I had to pretend that publishing my first book was all about champagne and celebrations. I researched how to give a good speech, an inspiring one. I learned that it was important to tell your story and allow your audience to feel your vulnerability. That thought was practically paralyzing. But the people that flock to this particular art retreat are a very special group. They're often seeking their own truth and deeper meaning. Maybe it was the ideal setting to reveal the imperfection of my life and shed light on how I was responding to my new status as both a published author and a single parent.

The night I held the microphone in my hand and shared the journey from manuscript to print was the moment I began reinventing my world. I explained that the process of writing a book is similar to the hero's journey. You had to be committed and champion your work, because the obstacles might be far greater than you ever imagined. I spoke of slaying dragons and upside-down rainbows that smiled upon you. I talked about symbols and meaning and the need to be your own hero. And in that moment, underneath the lights, I felt the shift toward a new life and a stronger self and the profound need to help others do the same.

The way forward is built on the reclaiming of who we have always been, our essence, and on recognizing who we are supposed to become. My vast experience with rescuing fabric ended up being a lifesaver when I needed my own rescuing. By focusing on the inherent best qualities of a material, I gain a sense of its potential. I know just how to transform it into the next iteration—which is always more amazing than its original incarnation. In a metaphorical way, people are woven together just like fabric—and can be reinvented by celebrating their strengths, recognizing their weaknesses, and honoring who they once were.

The projects that follow will see you through the next phase with strength and confidence. You can grow your own hope, frame your face in vitality, carry essential tools in style, become a superhero, and make enough feathers to grow your very own wings.

REINVENTION: A GUIDED MEDITATION

Before beginning each project, give yourself the gift of stillness. Listening and feeling where you are in the moment help bring awareness to your growth and focus to your transformation.

With gentle attention, sit comfortably yet upright. With intention, take several deep breaths and then allow your breath to be natural. See what it is like to relax as much as possible. Soften at the eyes. Try on a smile at the eyes and the mouth, reverberating down to the heart. A smile, even a slight upturn at the mouth, gives our nervous system an invitation to relax.

Chest open, belly soft, let your awareness return, again and again, to the sensations of your breath—the inflow and outflow. Let this breath be a kind of home base, a gateway to being here.

Whenever you notice that your thoughts have wandered to the past or the future, that is a moment of awareness—a homecoming. If it helps, consider placing your hand on your heart as a loving reminder that you can be home in any moment.

The times when things go well for us often point to the development of a more accepting attitude toward whatever we are experiencing in our lives—fear, anger, sadness, joy, relief, boredom, love. For all of us, the path of befriending our circumstances requires great gentleness and patience in the face of the deep and persistent tendency to think that something is wrong with us. It is this lack of compassion toward ourselves that imprisons and prevents us from living and loving fully. So when things are going well, this semblance of grace and ease with all that is arising doesn't come without careful (full of care) attention and practice in our life. Mostly it comes from cultivating a tender attitude toward ourselves.

When we begin to touch our own heart with loving-kindness, we discover that our heart is indeed limitless and can accommodate even great hardship. By cultivating warmth and gentleness for ourselves, joy arrives. It happens in the present moment of homecoming.

Scarflette

(I am growing)

The vitality of fresh leaves infuses this soft miniscarf and reminds you to look at each new day as an opportunity for growth and stretching. Use two T-shirts to make it reversible. What a wonderful opportunity to elevate a couple of well-loved shirts from a special time or person in your life. Choose them with intention.

HEART PROMPT

Before you begin, think about the lessons the season of springtime offers. After a time of darkness and deep cold, bare branches confidently unfurl their new leaves at the first taste of warmer weather. Have faith in your abilities to stretch and reach out even after a long winter of the soul.

1. Photocopy and cut out the template. Spread out a T-shirt and smooth out any wrinkles. Pin the template to the shirt parallel to the bottom hem and slightly above it (see illustration), with the short side aligned with the fold at the side of the shirt.
2. Cut out the first piece, being sure to cut through both layers and leaving the fold intact.
3. Turn the second T-shirt inside out and follow steps 1 and 2.
4. Unfold both pieces and place them together, wrong side to wrong side. Pin them in place. Using a sewing machine or needle and thread and a running stitch, topstitch around the perimeter of the entire scarflette. Stitch in the veins of the leaves.
5. Cut a 1-inch slit near the bottom of one of the leaves (see photograph).
6. Wrap the scarflette around your neck and insert one leaf through the slit.

Celebrate your own season of growth and expansion.

- **Scarflette template (see page 120)**
- **Scissors**
- **2 large cotton T-shirts with complementary colors**
- **Pins**
- **Needle and thread or sewing machine**

STEP 1

Growing Hope

(I am flourishing)

Planting a seed and watching it grow celebrate possibility and promise. You don't need a plot of land or even a backyard—a few cans sitting in a windowsill can provide many of the healing benefits of gardening. Add the unexpected element of a special word printed on the pots and you can cultivate anything: from "hope" to "trust."

HEART PROMPT

Consider the simplest needs of a plant—healthy soil, light, and water. What are your basic needs? What else might you require to thrive that you don't receive or insist upon? Are there steps you might take to ensure that your growth is supported?

MATERIALS

- **4 clean empty soup cans (labels removed)**
- **Measuring tape**
- **Scissors**
- **Scraps of linen, cotton, or burlap in a neutral color**
- **Needle and thread or sewing machine**
- **Hope template (page 121; optional)**
- **Freezer paper**
- **Pencil**
- **Craft knife and self-healing mat or old cookie sheet**
- **Iron and ironing board**
- **Textile paint**
- **Foam brush**
- **Potting soil**
- **Seeds (see planting suggestions)**
- **Water spray bottle**
- **Damp rag**

MAKE

1. First make a slipcover for each can: Measure the height of the can, then measure the length around the body of the can (the circumference) and add ¾ inch to this latter measurement. Cut four pieces of fabric with these measurements (for example, if your can were 5 inches high and 10 inches around, you would cut the pieces 5 inches high by 10¾ inches wide).

2. Fold each fabric rectangle in half width-wise, with the right sides touching. Sew a straight seam down the length side using a ½-inch seam allowance. Turn right side out and try on the slipcover. Pull a few threads from the top of the fabric to create a frayed edge.

3. Remove the slipcovers and flatten each with the seam centered in the back.

4. Select a four-letter word, such as *hope,* to be spelled by your cans. Prepare letter stencils by printing from a computer the letters of your word in your favorite font. Make sure each letter is approximately 1½ inches tall. The Hope template is an alternative to printing the letters.

5. Place the freezer paper shiny side down over the letters and trace them on the matte side of the paper. Make sure to leave lots of space around each letter, since they will be placed individually on each can. Use scissors to cut around each letter, allowing a minimum of 2 inches of paper on all sides of the letters. You will have four letters total, each centered on its own piece of paper. Carefully cut out each letter with a craft knife on a self-healing mat or an old cookie sheet.

6. Iron the letter stencils, shiny side down, onto the front center of each slipcover. Take care to place each letter at the same height from the bottom so that the word is positioned evenly when completed.

7. Apply textile paint to the paper stencil with the foam brush, then brush the paint from the paper onto the fabric—sweeping the color from the outside edges to the center of the letter. Allow the paint to dry. Pull off the paper and heat set each letter by flipping the slipcover over so the letter is face down and ironing the fabric briefly on high heat.

8. Fill each can with soil to about 1 inch from the top. Sprinkle seeds densely and evenly over the surface. Cover with a dusting of additional soil. Spray on just enough water to moisten the top of the soil. Clean up the outside of the can with a damp rag.

9. Slide the covers on and arrange the cans in a spot that gets a nice amount of light, such as a windowsill or a sunny shelf. Water the seeds regularly to keep the soil moist but not soggy. Misting the soil's surface while the seeds germinate is helpful.

Watch your garden grow!

PLANTING SUGGESTIONS

Wheat seeds grow quickly and look fresh and vital. You can give your wheatgrass a "haircut" when it gets really long.

Aromatic plants like lavender look beautiful and smell divine.

Plant a tea garden and include different kinds of mint and chamomile.

Make a mini-kitchen garden with culinary herbs and eat the words you grow.

Survival Satchel

(I am resourceful)

Being prepared for any of life's little mishaps is one response to the reality that we have very little control during challenging times. This carryall can be your everyday bag loaded with daily provisions, or it can be a wonderful holder for many of the tools created in this book. It's an ode to Clara Barton, the caregiver who founded the Red Cross. She carried a very similar satchel into battle or in the aftermath of natural disasters. She filled it with all of the comforts and necessities one might need—from bandages to jars of jam.

HEART PROMPT

Consider what you might include in an emotional-survival tool kit. These items don't all have to fit in your satchel, nor do they have to be tangible and accessible. Create your wish list of supplies and be sure to include at least one item for each of your senses.

MATERIALS

- **Wool army-blanket section measuring 13 × 32 inches**
- **Scissors**
- **Pins**
- **Needle and button thread or sewing machine**
- **Iron and ironing board**
- **Leather belt**
- **Leather punch**
- **Pencil**
- **Freezer paper**
- **Craft knife and self-healing mat**
- **Foam brush**
- **Textile paint**
- **Fabric scrap**

MAKE

1. If you haven't already, cut the blanket to the dimensions specified. There is no right side or wrong side for a wool blanket. Fold one of the 32-inch sides up by 12 inches to make the body of the bag. Pin the folded fabric in place. Cut a 1-inch square out of the bottom right and left corners at the fold.

2. Using a ½-inch seam allowance, sew straight down each side of the bag, from the top edge of the folded-up fabric to the top edge of the cut-out square. The top of each seam will receive a lot of stress from opening and closing the bag, so add a few extra stitches there for added strength.

3. Create the boxed corner by opening the square at the bottom so that the bag bottom and side meet along the 2-inch cut edge. Stitch this edge closed with another straight seam ½-inch from the edge. Repeat on the other side.

4. Turn the bag inside out. Fold the excess fabric over to create a front flap. You can skip to adding the strap at this point or finish the flap by hemming it. Either way works, since wool edges won't fray very much and can be left raw.

5. To hem the flap, press each side under by ½ inch. Finally, fold over the bottom of the flap ½ inch and press with an iron. Sew the folded hems in place just like the other sides.

6. Add the strap. You will be using the entire belt, including the buckle. Buckle the belt and slice it at least 5 inches below the buckle side. Use a leather hole puncher to

create four holes in a square formation near end of the strap. (The bag shown uses a belt with a double row of holes throughout, which eliminates the need for this step.) Using a needle and button thread, attach each end of the strap directly centered over the side seams about 1½ inches from the top. Create a stitched X by stitching back and forth diagonally through each hole.

7. Add a stencil to the flap if desired: Trace a drinking glass on the matte side of a 6-inch-square sheet of freezer paper. Cut out the entire circle, resulting in a square of freezer paper with a circle cut out of the center of it, and iron it shiny side down to the center of the flap. Cut out a shape or symbol of your choosing from another piece of freezer paper. Center it in the circular frame and iron it shiny side down. Using a foam brush, apply textile paint over the stencil in light layers. Allow the paint to dry, and then peel off the paper. Place a piece of fabric over the stencil and iron it on high heat to set the paint.

8. Fill your bag and know that whatever comes your way, you're that much more prepared.

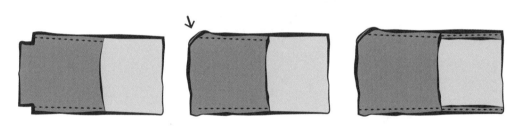

STEP 3

Power Poncho

(I am brave)

Here is an extra layer of warmth that is easy, effortless, and deceptively simple to make. I created my first poncho from a long circle dress I bought at a thrift store. My intention was to reduce it to a skirt. I got as far as cutting it, but the moment I pulled it over my head, I felt a transformation take place and kept it on my shoulders. A superhero cape was born. The soft drape of the jersey, combined with the circular pattern, created the subtle hint of wings each time I raised my arms. Whenever I wore it, I felt strong, bold, and quietly in charge. People took notice, and they wanted one too. I wore it constantly during a time when I needed a little extra courage and confidence. It gave me all of that, as well as being the perfect weight during seasonal transitions or even on chilly mornings before the house warmed up.

This version was designed just for you, with a built-in cowl that offers an elegant drape or a protective hood. Slip it on, raise your arms to the sky, and get ready to feel your inner superhero emerge.

HEART PROMPT

If you had secret powers, what would you want them to be? Are there strengths and skills that you don't recognize in yourself but others seem to see? What would happen if you owned them fully? Try them on for a day.

- Roll of paper for circle template (brown postal paper works well)
- Pencil
- Yardstick
- Jersey bedsheet (a single flat sheet is more than enough) or 2½ yards of 60-inch-wide fabric
- Pins
- Scissors
- Needle and button thread or sewing machine outfitted with a jersey needle

1. Use the circle-pattern-making technique (see page 115) to create a template for one-fourth of a 52-inch-diameter circle. Use 26 inches (the radius) as your measurement. There's no need for the full circle, as the template will be used on folded fabric. This measurement will create a small to medium-sized poncho. For something larger (or much smaller), find your "wingspan": measure from a little past your wrist to the hollow of your throat. My measurement is 26 inches.

2. Fold your fabric in half in the same manner that you folded the template paper. Place the right angle of the template along the folded sides. Place the curve toward the open sides. Pin the template in place.

3. Cut the jersey along the curve. Remove the pins. Do not unfold the fabric yet.

4. Make a quarter-circle template for a 7-inch-diameter circle, using 3½ inches (the radius) as your measurement. Pin the right angle of this template to the still-folded corner of your fabric. Cut along the curve. Unpin the template and set aside the larger circle and discard the smaller circle of fabric.

5. With the remaining uncut fabric, measure and cut a 28- × 22-inch rectangle. (The direction of the stretch isn't too important because this will be the cowl/hood.) Fold over the 28-inch side in half with right sides facing. Create a tube by sewing the 22-inch sides together with a ½-inch seam allowance with a needle and thread or a sewing machine. Turn the tube right side out.

6. Turn the circle of fabric wrong side out. Insert the tube

(right side out) into the hole in the center of the circle until the top edge is flush with the edge of the opening. Pin the top edge of the tube to the edge of the opening. Attach it by stitching around the top with a ½-inch seam allowance.

7. Turn the poncho right side out and toss it over your head, with the cowl seam at the back.

Feathered

(I am soaring)

Who doesn't delight in finding a feather at their feet? They are little gifts of hope and speak to us of lightness and flight. Feathers drop from the sky like messengers whispering permission to soar above the earthly matters that weigh us down. Their symbolism evokes a universal response that has the ability to free us from the heaviness of our internal struggles.

I was drawn to feathers over and over again during my most challenging times. I gathered feathers by the shore, found feathers on my walks, and collected feathers from my hens. I even began making my own. I carved feathered stamps and printed them on paper and fabric. Drawing each detail of a feather in ink and painting it in vivid watercolors became my evening meditation for some time.

This final offering is filled with the feathers I created during my journey, as well as a few I've made just for you. All of the projects below are starting points and call out for personal interpretation because the road to healing and transformation is unique for each person. You are on your way, and may these feathers inspire your wings to grow.

HEART PROMPT

If you created your own wings, where would they take you?

FEATHER MANDALA COLLAGE

This project is far more about process than product, and yet the end result can't help but be beautiful.

MATERIALS

- **Feather templates, photocopied, cut out, and painted (see pages 122–23)**
- **Double-sided tape**
- **Stretched canvas**
- **Glue**
- **Ephemera**
- **Paint and brushes**

MAKE

Arrange the feathers in a balanced circle or square. The process of creating mandalas is said to stabilize, integrate, and reorder our inner life. For a temporary and moveable design, adhere double-sided tape to the back of each feather and stick them to the canvas. For a more permanent piece, use white glue and collage an interesting background first with ephemera, paint, and paintbrushes.

PRINTING FEATHERS

For the projects here, I recommend photocopying the feather templates at the back of the book on card stock or thick art paper to increase their sturdiness. Add color with a wash of watercolors or colored pencils and then cut the feathers out with sharp scissors or a craft knife. Affirmations or inspiring quotes are easy additions: write them directly on the back or print them out in a small font on regular-weight printing paper. Use a glue stick to add them to the front or back of the feathers as you like.

FEATHER WREATH

A wreath is often associated with holidays. Make every day a celebration of healing with this feather wreath on display.

MAKE

Use a dinner plate to trace a circle on the cardboard. Trace a dessert plate in the center of that circle. Cut out each of the circles to create a wreath shape. Punch a hole at the top center and thread some ribbon through it to create a loop with which to hang the wreath. Adhere the feathers in layers with glue, with their quills pointing toward the center. Begin with the outside edge and add feathers until the desired fullness is reached.

MATERIALS

- **Plates, dinner and dessert sized**
- **Cardboard (a pizza box works well)**
- **Scissors**
- **Hole punch**
- **Ribbon**
- **Feather templates, photocopied, cut out, and painted (see pages 122–23)**
- **Glue**

A string of feathers is an eye-catching way to pay tribute to the work you are doing. This banner honors your self-worth.

MATERIALS

- Sharpies
- Feather templates, photo-copied, cut out, and painted (see pages 122–23)
- Clear tape
- Button thread

MAKE

With a Sharpie, write an affirmation on each feather, or write a letter on each feather to spell out one powerful affirmation. Tape each end of a long piece of thread to the wall. Tape the feathers to the thread, being sure to space them evenly. Leave your bunting on the wall or hang it in front of a window or over a doorway.

FEATHER MOBILE

The act of gathering materials and creating balance is the focus of this project. The result will be a beautiful piece of art to remind you to keep steady and level.

Tie a piece of fishing line or button thread around the quill of each feather. Add assorted bits to decorate the string. Tie each feathered strand individually to the driftwood or branch to achieve a balanced effect. Hang your beautiful mobile.

- Button thread or fishing line
- Feather templates, photo-copied, cut out, and painted (see pages 122–23)
- Beads, shells, and other bits from nature
- Driftwood or a pretty branch

Nourish: Sunrise Smoothie

There are moments when we all wish we could be transported to a tropical island. That's rarely a reality, but you can blend a bit of paradise and pour it into a glass without leaving your kitchen. This is my favorite weekend smoothie, but it also works whenever I need a minivacation.

INGREDIENTS

- 1½ cups coconut water
- 1 cup fresh or frozen mango, peaches, pineapple
- 1 banana
- 1 pinch bee pollen
- 1 handful frozen strawberries

MAKE

Add everything but the strawberries to a blender and mix them together. Pour half of this mixture into a glass. Add the strawberries to the remaining smoothie and blend until they are incorporated. Pour the rest of the smoothie into the glass on top of the first batch. Use a straw to marbleize the smoothie.

TOOLS AND TECHNIQUES

Almost every project included in this book requires only basic tools and beginner skills. Here I've included a list of my favorite tools, but I recommend using whatever works well for you.

TOOLS FREQUENTLY USED

Scissors. You should have at least three pairs. Designate one for fabric and another for paper; the third can be all-purpose. Label them so you know which is which. Dull blades result when their uses are mixed.

Iron and ironing board. Because I heat set so many projects, I keep the steam component that comes with most irons empty of water. I keep a spray bottle handy for when moisture is needed to reduce wrinkles.

Button thread. This heavy-weight thread is the most durable and easy to use for hand sewing. Its silky finish keeps it from tangling, while its strength ensures that your stitches will last. It's widely available at sewing and craft stores (though it comes in a limited palette). I use it for everything from sewing to mobiles and bunting.

Needles with eyes big enough for button thread. Look for needles with a long eye and a sharp tip.

Craft knife and extra blades. Also called an X-Acto knife or a pen blade—they are fantastic for paper and cardboard cutting. I've been known to sharpen my pencils with one, too.

Self-healing mats. These mats are almost indispensable if you're using a blade for cutting. Find them in craft stores and in quilting sections of fabric shops. In a pinch, an old cookie sheet works well, but they dull blades quickly.

Rulers. Here are suggestions for two favorites: a quilter's acrylic ruler and a yardstick, which is handy not only for measuring straight lines but also for creating circle templates (as I describe below).

Glue. Basic white glue can be used throughout the projects in this book, but the addition of glue sticks, Mod Podge, and a hot-glue gun is helpful.

Paint. Inexpensive acrylic craft paints are all that are needed, along with a set of watercolors. Large projects like the Blank Canvas use house paint. Textile paint can be purchased at most craft and large fabric stores.

Paintbrushes. It's nice to have an assortment of brushes, but standard foam brushes can be used for many of the projects.

Freezer paper. This paper is indispensible for stenciling on fabric surfaces. Find it in the aluminum foil and plastic wrap section of the grocery store. One side is matte and the other is shiny; the shiny side will adhere to fabric when heated with an iron.

TECHNIQUES
Hand Sewing with a Running Stitch

The running stitch is the one most people learn first and is the simplest to use for the projects in this book. Begin with a piece of button thread that is twice the length of your arm. Put one end of the thread through the eye of the needle and pull it until it is centered. Tie the ends together with a double knot. Insert the needle on the underside of the fabric, or where you want the knot to be placed. Pull the needle all the way through and drop it back down into the fabric, creating the first stitch. Continue this rhythm of the needle dipping in and out of the fabric. The spacing and evenness of the stitches determines the strength and tidiness of the seam. Generally, smaller stitches with little space between them are your goal. Create a line with a pencil where your seam should be and sew directly over it to make even and level stitches without stress.

Creating a Circle Template

This method of creating a circle template is used in both the Power Poncho and the Wise Cap. Making a perfect circle is easy—all you need is three simple tools and these two terms from geometry class:

• **Diameter:** the measurement directly across the center of a circle
• **Radius:** half of the diameter

1. Gather a pencil, a ruler (or a yardstick if it's a big circle), and a piece of paper that fits the diameter of your desired circle size. Fold the paper in half, then turn it one-quarter turn clockwise and fold it in half again. It's now folded in quarters. Place the paper so that the two folded sides are on the left and the bottom.
2. Mark the length of the radius on the left and bottom sides with your ruler.
3. Place the ruler's length flush with the left side of the paper and align the bottom edge of the ruler with the paper's bottom edge. Keep the bottom left corner of the ruler exactly where the paper's two sides meet and slowly rotate the ruler from one radius to the other. Mark dots every ½ inch along the way.

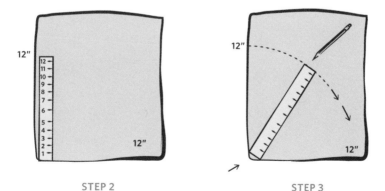

STEP 2   STEP 3

4. Connect the dots and cut along the line they create. When you open up the paper, you'll have the circle size you were hoping for.

Freezer-Paper Stencil Printing Basics

The following simple technique creates crisp mono prints akin to silk screen in result but uses minimal equipment.

1. Draw your design directly on the matte side of the paper.
2. Cut out the design from the paper with a craft knife on a self-healing mat to create a stencil on the paper.
3. Place the stencil on the fabric with the shiny side down. When it's positioned just where you desire, iron it in place with medium to high heat for a few seconds.
4. Before you paint your stencil place something under the fabric to protect your surface. An old cereal box works well. Add a small amount of textile paint to the paper near the edges of the design. Gently sweep the paint to the center of the fabric and cover it evenly with paint.
5. Allow the paint to dry and then lift off the paper.
6. Heat set the design with an iron by placing a light piece of fabric (such as muslin) over the paint and placing the iron on top for about 30 seconds.

TEMPLATES

NAUTICAL NECKLACE

Earth Care

- Spend some simple time in the garden doing seasonal chores
- Choose one bed to focus on. Only one.
- Tend the soil as you would a child.
- Weeds can be helped out, rather than yanked.
- Add nutrients or water lovingly.
- This is not about getting work done quickly.
- Simply take some time to nurture and be grateful for the soil that feeds you.

Watercolor Mandala

- Gather: paint, H_2O, brushes, and watercolor paper
- Find a comfy spot near a window or outside.
- Remind yourself that you are calming the mind, not creating a masterpiece.
- Begin with a circle in the center of the paper.
- Add 4 matching shapes to the perimeter of the circle - 1 for each direction.
- Continue adding shapes/colors in concentric rings.
- However you do this is the RIGHT way!

Walking Awareness

- Prepare a foot bath with warm H_2O and bubbles or essential oils.
- Sit back and soak feet until H_2O cools.
- Dry and massage each foot with oil.
- Bring your loving attention to these hard working and often neglected soles
- Thank them for their daily gifts.
- Take a SLOW, shoeless walk outside (if weather and environment permit)
- Take only one step for each inhale and exhale.
- In this moment, you have no where to get to. Enjoy the pace.

Cloud Gazing

- choose a day with blue skies and puffy, white clouds.
- Lie down on a soft patch of grass or a blanket.
- Look up.
- Allow your breath to slow and deepen.
- Notice clouds drifting by
- Invite your thoughts to float away with the clouds.
- Drifting, gazing, breathing

Steam Bath

- Play soothing music and insert ear buds, if possible.
- Add a handful of dried herbs to a bowl of steaming H_2O. (lavender & chamomile)
- Sit comfortably with face over the steaming bowl.
- Drape a towel over your head to create a tent.
- Allow the sensations to envelope you.

SCARFLETTE

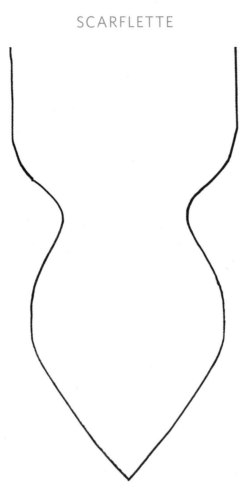

ENLARGE 110%

HOPE

RESOURCES FOR SUPPORT
DURING LIFE'S TRANSITIONS

BOOKS

Anam ara: A Book of Celtic Wisdom, John O'Donohue

The Book of Awakening, Mark Nepo

Broken Open: How Difficult Times Help Us Grow, Elizabeth Lesser

Finding Inner Courage, Mark Nepo

The Geography of Loss, Patti Digh

The Gifts of Imperfection, Brené Brown

Happiness Is an Inside Job: Practicing for a Joyful Life, Sylvia Boorstein

The Journey from Abandonment to Healing, Susan Anderson

Loving-Kindness: The Revolutionary Art of Happiness, Sharon Salzburg

The Tao of Psychology: Synchronicity and Self, Jean Shinoda Bolen

This I Know, Susannah Conway

When Thing Fall Apart: Heart Advice for Difficult Times, Pema Chödrön

Wild Comfort: The Solace of Nature, Kathleen Dean Moore

WEBSITES AND AUDIO

Guided meditations with Tara Brach, tarabrach.com

SouLodge with Pixie Lighthorse, pixielighthorse.com

Soundstrue.com

Deva Premal, all recordings are recommended

SUPPORTIVE TOOLS

Rescue Remedy pastilles
Inquiry Cards from inquirycards.com
Aromatherapy and flower essences from annawingfield.com
Lavender from frontiercoop.com

ABOUT THE CONTRIBUTORS

ELLEN ABRAMS has more than fifteen years of clinical experience as a marriage and family therapist in community mental-health clinics, in hospices, and in private practice. Her work is grounded in a deep faith that loss, unexpected change, or difficult transitions can offer opportunities for growth and change. She runs trauma-informed mindfulness groups as a place to explore oneself through the lens of kindness and to develop, with support and connection, practices that cultivate a positive sense of self, equanimity, and nourishment.

PIXIE LIGHTHORSE is a tribal mother of the world working her own brand of magic. She practices ritual and ceremony with an indigenous influence, along with a modern application for divine feminine vitality. She believes that it's up to women to heal themselves and change the world. Her capacity for nurture, compassion, vulnerable strength, wildness, ferocity and mysticism guides her as she walks with thousands of women on a path for transformation. Her mission is to see every woman in a sacred circle in her lifetime. She created SouLodge.com to fulfill this vision.

ANNA WINGFIELD is an aromatherapist and flower-essence practitioner—petals and potions are the medium with which she creates personal-care products. Her goal is to support and possibly help heal the hearts that use them—to make the journey more pleasurable in even the tiniest way by a sumptuous sniff or scintillating heart quiver. Her aim is to touch the earth gently and make a difference at the same time.

ABOUT THE AUTHOR

MAYA PAGÁN DONENFELD'S distinct designs utilize sustainable resources and fibers while weaving in elements from the natural world. She finds the imperfection of handmade items endlessly inspiring and seeks out simple, and often humble, materials to transform into useful items of beauty. She is the author of *Reinvention: Sewing with Rescued Materials.*

Maya is passionate about encouraging others to find their unique creative voice and gain confidence in their own capable hands through her workshops and lifestyle blog, *maya*made.* Her work has been featured in dozens of books and magazines.

Maya lives with her two children in an old farmhouse down a country road in the Finger Lakes region of New York State.